BENEATH THE CLOUDS

Further details of Poppyland Publishing titles can be found at
www.poppyland.co.uk
where clicking on the 'Support and Resources' button
will lead to pages specially compiled to support this title.

Beneath the
Clouds

A Social History of
the US Army Air Forces in the UK
1942–45

by Jackie Stuart

POPPYLAND
PUBLISHING

First published 2012
ISBN 978 0 94614894 3

Published by Poppyland Publishing, Cromer, NR27 9AN

Designed and typeset in 11 on 14 pt Charlotte Book by Watermark, Cromer, NR27 9ER

Front cover picture: A crew in the 390th Bomb Group Framlingham

Printed by Lightning Source

Contents

Hitler built a fortress around Europe, but he forgot to put a roof on it.

FRANKLIN D. ROOSEVELT

Preface

This book started as an undergraduate dissertation. I lived in Cambridge at the time and many veterans were returning to the UK to visit their old air bases and to see British people they knew from the war. The veterans were very happy to discuss their wartime social memories with me and many of them gave my address to other veterans who kindly sent me contemporary letters, diaries, photographs. They also sent me audio tapes telling me quite a lot about their wartime memories. Also, some veterans invited me to stay with them in America so I could do further research with their friends. I attended several States to visit them. To all of them, and to my British informants, I am grateful; their names are listed on pages 152–3.

1

Arrival and First Impressions

Off we go into the wild blue yonder
Climbing high into the sun,
Here they come, zooming to meet our thunder;
At 'em boys, give 'er the gun
GIVE 'ER THE GUN! Hey!
Down we dive, spouting our flames from under,
Off with one helluva roar;
We live in fame
Or go down in flame, HEY!
Nothing can stop the Army Air Corps.
ARMY AIR FORCE OFFICIAL SONG – WORLD WAR 2

The idea of life in the United States Army Air Forces (USAAF) was hugely seductive to many of the young men of America, and propaganda songs such as the one above contrived to stoke the flames of youthful enthusiasm. The wave of patriotism that swept across America immediately after the devastating Japanese attack on Pearl Harbor on 7th December 1941 brought forth masses of volunteers for aerial combat duty. Many of these positions were offered on a voluntary basis as the very nature of the job demanded high levels of fitness, energy and motivation. Aerial combat appealed to young men in particular because they needed adventure and excitement,

9

but even more importantly it provided them with an opportunity to shake off the deprivation and gloom of the Great Depression which still cast a pall over American life. It was a job that was highly respected within the community. Their USAAF uniforms and badges were worn with masculine pride and a conviction of moral superiority.

The arrival of the Americans in England was known as the Friendly Invasion. They had been before, when America joined the First World War in 1917 and United States soldiers came to Britain on their way to fight in France. The Second World War was different in that it included the Air War which meant that many more 'friendly invaders' arrived. They were described by some of the British as brash, self-opinionated, over-confident and undisciplined. However, it was also noted that they were lively, good-humoured, kind and generous. In both cases, the Yanks were welcomed as their very presence brought a pleasurable reassurance to the war weary British that victory would now be theirs. In both wars they brought optimism, new blood and the vigorous will to win.

There was a major difference though between these young men and the military of their fathers' generation. The inter-war years had seen substantial and far reaching changes in combat. The aeroplane now played a pivotal role, having been perfected into a machine capable of delivering weapons of such terrible magnitude that the word 'front' had little meaning now that battle zones extended as far as an aeroplane could fly.

Combat crews of the 1940s were close units and had to rely on each others' various skills to maximise their safety. They also had to rely on non-combatants who serviced their aircraft and packed their parachutes as well as those who dealt with the general administration and logistics of the base.

Many of the support personnel on base were draftees (known as enlisted men – EMs), but they too were an important part of the team and the majority did their job with pride and dedication. Although flying duty was voluntary, many ground staff had also volunteered, offering their specialist services or their willingness to undertake specialist training.

From the age of 18 all young men were subject to the Government draft. Even before Pearl Harbor, Army Air Force propagandists were visiting High Schools on recruitment drives promising candidates that they could finish their education before entry into the service. Unfortunately, this concession was waived once war was declared and many young men left High School for the war prior to graduating; several of these were potential officer material. Al Jones, later to become a bombardier, remembered that the opportunity to become a flier was too good to resist and that 'a commission was socially important'. Others had carefully selected the USAAF after a childhood spent dreaming about flying in an aeroplane. The educational requirements were lowered when the US entered the war and this made it possible for more young men to fly in combat. One pilot remembered that when he heard he had been accepted for flight training, he was 'as happy as a pig in slop'. He admitted he gave little thought to the fact that one day he would find himself in combat. Some were not accepted for reasons of health, weight or height, but many determined candidates were successful on a second attempt. One prospective pilot passed the mental examination but failed the physical on account of being ten pounds underweight for his height. He was told that he could try again in two weeks if he could put on ten pounds in weight. On the morning of the physical he drank five pints of milk, ate ten pounds of bananas and didn't visit the toilet. His determination paid off and he weighed in at just the required weight.

A young man who was to become a gunner failed the physical due to a slight heart murmur. He was particularly unhappy at this outcome, as he had persuaded five of his friends to join also and they were all accepted. Complete rest for a week and a second attempt got this man through.

Bob Banta was a gunner at Framlingham, Suffolk, and kept a journal throughout the war; he was very pleased to be accepted into the USAAF. However, he said: 'I was very naïve because I was astonished to find that I was being shot at when in combat!'

Psychology for the Fighting Man, a Government publication prepared 'for the fighting man himself' in 1943, attempted to explain the process of selection and why the Army Air Forces were so popular:

> *In . . . an interview, the examiner tries to find out what the soldier's interests are. He goes beyond mere preferences, finding out whether or not the interests are based on the man's deep-rooted unchangeable likes and dislikes . . . For example, about three-fourths of the drafted men would like to go into the Air Corps. Of these, three-fourths want to be pilots. Why? Most men have heard much*

Bob Banta, Gunner, 390th Bomb Group, Framlingham. (USAF)

about the exploits of ace pilots. They hear considerably less about the adventures of the bombardier, of the Signal Corps man, of the man with the rifle. Flying is popular, even among those who have never flown . . . Yet often a man may give the Army Air Force as his preference because he is really keen about aviation. He may have been around flying fields since he was a small boy. He may have built model planes. Such a man would be willing, the interviewer discovers, to do any kind of work to get into the Army Air Forces. He has been studying mathematics and physics in school to fit himself for this job. He wants to be a pilot, but he would gladly be a navigator, bombardier or gunner – anything, just so he gets a job in the air. His skill in mathematics added to his interest may make him a man the Army Air Forces need for a navigator . . . Another man may give the same preference but knows nothing about aviation or engines or planes, dislikes mechanical work and hates mathematics. But he has been seeing movies and reading books in which a pilot is the dashing hero. He wants adventure and action. But his hobby is game shooting and he is a good shot. Other things he says all point to the fact that he would be successful and well placed in the infantry, that he would get to be an expert ground soldier.

Once in the Army Air Force, these men had no control over where they would be posted and none of those who arrived in England knew in advance that this was where they would serve. As the aeroplanes were manufactured in the USA, they had to be flown to Britain, mostly by the crews who would subsequently take them into battle. For reasons of security, the destination was not revealed until after they had been in the air for an hour by which time they were allowed to open an envelope which would reveal their flight route and destination.

Ground support staff and replacement combat crews made the journey by ocean liners such as the *Queen Mary* (which was on return Lend-Lease to the US Government). These luxury liners, now troop carriers, zig-zagged their way across the Atlantic to avoid being torpedoed by the German U-boats. Around 12,000 men were crammed into all corners, sleeping in shifts with the dubious luxury of a bunk every two or three nights. Feeding these men with limited resources was indeed a problem, and it was not remembered fondly. Chuck Galian, an aircraft mechanic, vividly recalled that trip:

Everyone, including the crew, was ill. The second day out I decided to try to keep some food down. The Mess Halls were below decks and the odor was terrible. We stood at long tables to eat. I stood there looking at the tray of food and argued with my stomach about its ability to keep anything down.

12

All the time was boat was pitching and rolling . . .

*There were about 20 of us standing at this table, all with the same problem–
ill, hungry and disgusted. Some guy at the end of the table threw up. Now
there was a rim around the edge of the table to prevent things falling off.
Every time the ship moved up and down, the mess slid from one end of the
table to another. We all headed for the door and fresh air. My buddy said: 'If
I have to be this sick coming back, I think I'll stay over there.'*

Leroy Kuest, a Ground Crew Chief, remembered his journey across the
Atlantic:

*I sailed out of New York on the Queen Elizabeth in May 1943. There were
15,000 men on board, all Army Air Force ground crew. All furniture had
been removed. Our barracks bags were all put in the swimming pool. State
rooms had three decker wooden bunks to accommodate 18 personnel. We
were not allowed to open port holes so it got hot and stuffy. We only slept
one night there. The rest of the time we slept on the floor in the hallways.
We zig-zagged changing course every 9 minutes as that was the time it took
a submarine to line up on target. After six days we docked at Greenock in
Scotland, then took a train to Earls Colne.*

GIs ARRIVING IN BRITAIN. *(USAF via Frank Halm)*

13

In 1945, Staff Sergeant Gordon Hunsberger wrote home to his family and included information about his arrival in England two years earlier on the *Queen Elizabeth*.

The ship was tremendous in size . . . The restriction on space was pitiful . . . eight of us in a room about as big as our bathroom . . . Our meals on the ship were terrible consisting mostly of greasy foods . . . After sailing for many days there were rumours going around that we were going to England.

Peter Ardizzi, a Ground Sergeant, recalled that his 329th Service Squadron

arrived by troop train to Kamp Kilmer, New Jersey. It was a staging area and part of the New York Port of Embarkation. Troops were quartered there in preparation for transport to the European Theatre of Operations. From Kilmer we were lined up in single file with our barrack bags to board the Queen Mary. On board I was assigned to Stateroom 'A' with seven of my fellow soldiers. There were eight of us on two man bunks made of plywood that were highly polished with lacquer and no side rails. We spent the first 24 hours on deck and the next 24 hours below in our Stateroom. This meant that there were sixteen men sharing one room. We had two meals a day which I would like to forget. The best sleep we had was sleeping on deck wedged somewhere where we could not roll over. There were no showers or water in the cabin. We lived on one canteen cup of water daily. One of our cabin buddies, who was short, got the best rest by sleeping in the tub and therefore did not have to go topside every 24 hours. One night on deck, I woke up and questioned a soldier next to me as how high the spray was. A voice in the dark informed me that we were sleeping in the rain. We could not sleep in the Stateroom because at night the ship sped up in a zig-zag course sliding us off the plywood bed onto the floor. The Queen Mary could outrun any German submarine.

Frank Halm, a B17 pilot, was part of a replacement crew that arrived in the UK in 1944. He recalled being shipped over the Atlantic on the *Dominion Monarch*. This was a former luxury first class liner that was requisitioned by the British Government to act as a troopship. It appears though that this ship was no longer a luxury liner, but one of basic accommodation.

Whether arriving by sea or aeroplane, few were disappointed to find that England was their destination. Jim Sheller, a B17 pilot, had to make an emergency landing at a private airfield in the USA after being airborne over an hour and finding their orders were for England. Whilst waiting for the aircraft to be checked by the military, James's crew went shopping. They had heard 'how the British girls were deprived of nice things and dutifully loaded up with necessary bait such as lipstick, silk stockings, face powder and perfume.'

The main port for disembarking was Greenock, Scotland, and the GIs were often thrilled at the warm reception they received. The novelist John Steinbeck, who was a journalist in the 1940s, came over to England on a troopship and wrote home to his newspaper as noted in his book *Once There Was a War*:

> After docking, an astonishing thing happens. A band of pipers marches out in kilts, with bagpipes and drums and the swingy march of pipers. The harsh skirling cuts through the air. The most military, the most fighting music in the world. Our men crowd the rail, the band approaches, drums banging, pipes squealing and, as they draw abreast, the soldiers break into a great cheer. They may not like the harsh music; it takes time to like it; but something of the iron of the music goes into them. Our men, in some deep way, feel honoured. The music has stirred them. This is a different war from the one of training camps and strategy at post exchanges.
>
> From the deck the men can see the roofless houses, the burned-out houses and the piles of rubble where the bombs have fallen. They have seen pictures of this and have read about it, but that was pictures and reading. It wasn't real . . .

The local children, many of whom had never tasted an orange or a banana, soon learned that Greenock railway station was the place to be when the Yanks came into Britain, although a navigator who was married with a pregnant wife at home found this rather disturbing:

> As we waited for the train to move, it seemed like hundreds of young children lined up along the tracks. The guys began throwing out candy, oranges and apples. This almost created a riot as the children fought each other for these goodies. I felt a little sad watching as the GIs cheered for certain of these children as opposed to others. Some of us tried throwing things to some of the smaller kids while the others scrambled.

This train journey south was often a memorable experience too. British trains were slow; they were unheated in order to save fuel and were often dirty because labour was needed elsewhere. If the GIs arrived after dark, they would have been immediately introduced to the blackout – no street lighting anywhere, dimmed headlamps on cars and bikes, kerbstones and steps painted white. Some organisers of troop movements anticipated problems

A SHORT GUIDE TO

GREAT BRITAIN

WAR DEPARTMENT
Washington, D. C.

arising
from the black-
out and Bill Anderson, a ground
crew man, remembered that they had a number
chalked in white on the back of their helmets. He was number
129 and he needed to follow number 130. Hopefully, no one would get lost on
the journey, but if they did, it would become evident almost immediately.

The blackout was only one of many new experiences to come. The men of
the USAAF were mostly young and had never been away from home before,

and certainly not abroad. They were consequently somewhat unsophisti-cated and untutored in the ways of the world. The US Government clearly anticipated that misunderstandings and mistrust would only provide a negative influence in the war effort and it therefore seemed expedient to educate each side as to the little foibles of the other. For the education of the GIs, in 1942 the US War and Navy Departments jointly produced a small booklet, *A Short Guide to Great Britain*, which was handed to all in-coming servicemen. Both governments would have been aware that clashes between the Americans and the British would be disastrous for morale and the booklet aimed to provide the Americans with simple codes of behaviour as well as points of reference. This booklet also highlighted the main areas of concern, and although only 5" x 4" in dimensions and consisting of 31 pages, it did a remarkably good job for the men that read it.

The Yanks knew that England was small, but few realised how small in comparison with the United States. The *Short Guide* pointed this out, add-ing that 'no part of England is more than a hundred miles from the sea'. It also tried to prepare the men for their first impression of war-torn Britain:

> *At home in America you were in a country at war. Since your ship left port, however, you have been in a war zone. You will find that all Britain is a war zone and has been since September 1939. All this has meant great changes in the British way of life.*

> *Every light in England is blacked out every night and all night. Every signpost has come down and barrage balloons have gone up. Grazing land is now ploughed for wheat, and flower beds turned into vegetable gardens.*

The journey south took men through a variety of English landscapes. They travelled miles through the heart of industrial England in the north, down to the flat agricultural areas of eastern England towards the airfields designated for the use of the United States Army Air Forces. Many of these men had preconceived ideas of what England would be like, such as coast-to-coast built-up areas and no greenery. What they actually found came as a pleasant surprise. Few had expected so many green fields and pastures and discovered the country to be neat, orderly and small. One GI said it reminded him of a child's playground! The fields were not geometrical as in the USA, but a patchwork pattern that was shaped by ancient boundaries dating back many hundreds of years.

John A. Appleby, a ground crew man who was based in Suffolk and au-thor of *Suffolk Summer*, noted quite shrewdly that 'East Anglia is considered rather remote and backward by the rest of England,' which was probably due, he felt, to the fact that 'it is a sort of hump on the East Coast and one does not pass through it on his way to somewhere else'. However, he was immediately taken with its distinctive beauty:

The American eye is struck first of all by the dazzling greenness of the fields and by the beauty of the hedgerows . . . green; green beyond anything I had ever seen at home.

Often, the men's first and highly unofficial desire was to let their family at home know that they were in England. Of course, this was strictly against military regulations, but there were ways of getting around this problem. One man wrote a card home stating: 'Well, I've arrived and when I can, I will visit Grandma's birthplace.' This was innocent enough, but some were less cautious. A young gunner purchased a book of poems and he posted this home with a handwritten note about his destination which he pushed down into the spine. He remembered that his sister was as devious as he, because she found the note.

The German propaganda programme did its best to compromise the emotional security of the Americans during their stay in England. They blatantly played on the fact that the men were young and had left wives and sweethearts at home. A female voice, known as 'Axis Sally', would tell the men that the draft dodgers were at home with their girls. Popular American songs such as 'Home on the Range' were played over the radio interspersed with pleas for the men to go home, as they should not be fighting for England. Perhaps the most disturbing of all radio propagandists was the infamous Lord Haw Haw, who regularly welcomed Americans to their new base, naming the individual group. A bomber pilot wrote home in 1944:

Am listening to the German propaganda program run by a gal named Midge. She puts on a very entertaining program. The news comments being nothing short of hilarious, especially when they comment on operations we know about.

Sooner or later came payday and the GIs would be subjected to the complexities of British coinage. Britain did not operate on a decimal system at that time, but instead had twelve pennies to each shilling (a shilling was commonly known as a 'bob') and twenty shillings to the pound. There was also an odd variety of coins, including a threepenny bit (a small thick twelve-sided coin), a sixpence (a small silvery coin – a 'tanner'), and half a crown, which was worth two shillings and sixpence (an eighth of a pound in value). The two-shilling coin was also known as a florin. Unfortunately, the complication did not stop there. There was also in circulation another kind of threepence, small and silvery, which was similar to the sixpence. These were in the process of being phased out, but were still fairly commonplace at the time. Goods in shops were often priced in guineas, with a value of one pound and one shilling, or twenty-one shillings. However, guinea coins no longer existed (they ceased to be minted after 1813), which just added to the confusion.

The Americans also had to remember that a pound was worth just over four dollars and came in note form, as did ten shillings. British notes and coins were generally much larger than American currency and Chuck Galian remembered that to him, a £5 note (much bigger than a modern £5 note) 'looked like a High School diploma!' American wallets were designed to hold dollar bills and British notes had to be folded many times to be fitted in. Loose change was a problem as pennies were larger than a quarter and halfpennies were about the same size as a quarter. Because the system was so confusing, men offered a pound note for everything and accumulated small change in large amounts. Robert Arbib in his book *Here We are Together* recalled the first time he changed a pound note and when he put the change in his pocket he found himself 'with a slight list to starboard'.

The *Short Guide* produced a table of British currency and advised its readers not to be critical of this unfamiliar coinage:

> *The British are used to this system and they like it, and all your arguments that the American decimal system is better won't convince them. They won't be pleased to hear you call it 'funny money' either. They sweat hard to get it and they won't think you smart or funny for mocking at it.*

Much of the small change the men accumulated found its way to local children or beggars. Doris Foster, a pub landlady in Hertfordshire, recalled that at the end of the evening there would always be large numbers of pennies and halfpennies on the bar counter, left by those GIs who considered this small change not worth bothering with. She put a large jar on the bar and asked them to throw their unwanted coins into it. When £25 had been collected, the money was used to re-seat the Catholic Church in the local town of Royston, because so many of her American customers were Catholic.

The value of British money was always underestimated. A pound note was generally seen as having the same value as the American dollar, which in turn, led to much overspending. The GI earned relatively much more than his British counterpart of similar rank, so everything was cheaper for the Americans. This soon settled into a situation where the GI had more money than he actually needed in Britain, although many servicemen purchased American war bonds, invested in savings accounts, and continued to financially support the family at home. Harry Slater, a co-pilot, recalled his feelings when he was first allowed off base:

We never knew how much we were paying for fish and chips, beer etc., and really we didn't care much at the time because it was just one thing in a series of new experiences.

A further new experience was the British telephone kiosk, quite different from those in America. Money would be inserted for a three-minute call and the number was then dialled. When the call was answered, the caller needed to press button 'A' which dropped the money into the box and allowed the caller's voice to be heard. If there was no reply, button 'B' was pressed and the money returned in full. This system caused much hilarity, as well as confusion, among the Americans. In 1944 Jim Johnson, a Technical Sergeant newly arrived from the USA, reflected on his first experience with the telephone:

I had trouble getting the number I wanted, so I called the operator. She asked me to insert the money into the box and when the number answered, she told me to 'press button I'. Now, I looked everywhere for a button 'I', but I could only find a button A and B. After some confusion, it became apparent that I was speaking to a telephone operator with a strong Cockney accent. Her button 'I' was in fact button 'A'!

An aeroplane crew chief recalled with humour that when he or his friends found it difficult to attract the attention of someone, they would say loudly 'Please press button A.'

The slowness of the British telephone system was irritating to the Americans and one frustrated General's Aide asked the telephone operator 'How's about it Dearie. Do I have to marry you to get a connection?' (Redding and Leyshon, *Skyways to Berlin*).

England may well have appeared slow and old fashioned to many of these newcomers, but for the time being, it was their home.

2

Settling into the Base

A Nissen Hut is not a difficult thing to build. You put down a rectangle of concrete for a floor, you place spanning arched ribs across the longer dimensions, bracing them with longitudinal stays. You cover the inside and outside of these ribs with thin sheets of corrugated steel. You seal up the ends with bricks, wood or concrete. A couple of windows and a door at each end, and you are ready to take up residence. (ROBERT S. ARBIB)

A small percentage of Headquarters USAAF personnel lived and worked in the relative luxury of buildings such as the requisitioned Girls' School in High Wycombe, Berkshire, in the centre of England. Several veterans continued to remember with amusement a bell above the beds with a notice that read: 'Ring Once for Mistress.' However, the majority of men lived and worked on the hastily built air bases where the main features of life consisted of keeping warm and dry in the British winter.

The ground staff were always the first to arrive, needing time to prepare the working part of the base for the aircraft arrivals. The actual building work was undertaken by contractors to the British Government, but in many cases this work was still in progress when the first men arrived and some needed to sleep in tents. Tents did continue to provide some accommodation on air bases throughout the war when necessary.

Once the building constructions were completed, men could move in and make themselves as comfortable as possible. Living accommodation varied considerably from base to base, but generally consisted of a series of

Nᴉssᴇɴ Hᴜᴛs ᴀᴛ Rᴏᴜɢʜᴀᴍ Aᴉʀ Bᴀsᴇ 1944. *(Frank Halm)*

Nissen Huts in assorted sizes. These were not unfamiliar to the Yanks because the same type of building was manufactured in the USA at Quonset Point, Rhode Island. Consequently they were known as 'Quonset Huts'.

Despite the Spartan conditions, the men of the Army Air Forces knew they were better off than the infantry who were living in foxholes and they reminded themselves of this fact from time to time. However, living conditions on the bases presented them with many problems and minimal comforts – one of these problems was the uninvited wildlife as recalled by gunner Dan O'Keefe:

> *Mice scampered around between the sheets of metal keeping us awake most nights. They made nests in our clothing which we hung from wires over our beds, and they got into any edibles we had even though we hung these precious items from strings. Mice often got into food parcels from home.*

Frank Halm, a B17 pilot, remembered hearing mice above him between the roof and the ceiling of his Nissen Hut:

> *I recall someone had chewed a bit off a Hershey chocolate bar (they were rationed). I considered throwing the bar away, but on consideration I broke off the chewed part and ate the rest of the bar.*

The following account by Bill Anderson, a ground crew man who was sleeping under canvas, makes the mouse problem appear rather tame:

> *We were all asleep one night and all of a sudden I woke up and felt something*

walking around on top of my blanket down near my feet. The first thing I thought of was that a cat had got in somehow and jumped on my bed. I let him walk around and when he got up near my waist, I swung my arm real hard and knocked him clean across the tent. I got up and turned on the light and to my surprise it wasn't a cat, but a very large rat. By this time everyone in the tent was awake, so we quickly disposed of the rat and went back to sleep.

Nissen huts had very poor lighting with only two or three lights overhead in each hut.

Due to the cold, damp climate in England, rain quickly turned to mud making getting around the base difficult and unpleasant. The 445th Bomb Group History noted that

King Mud was the outstanding element that the base has had to do battle with. In the early days it was worth your life to get off the beaten path. The boys went around singing: 'It always rains in England, at least once every day, and always rains on Sunday, because it has more time.' This was to the tune of 'There'll Always Be an England.' Around the middle of January, the base utilities began putting in walks and paving between the main building and the Mess Halls . . . since this time no missing personnel have been reported.

LATRINE AT ROUGHAM AIR BASE. *(Frank Halm)*

Leroy Kuest remembered that during the winter of 1944 'all our water was frozen up for two weeks in the wash houses and latrines. We had to use the slit trenches behind our planes for our ablutions.'

Barrack life was generally a segregated life with regard to rank and job. Officers and enlisted men of the ground echelon lived separately, as did the combat men, but status rarely influenced comfort any further than the number of men allocated to each hut. Mostly officers slept in single storey accommodation and enlisted men in double bunks. However, this was largely dictated by the base itself and what was available.

The men who lived on the few ex-RAF bases were a little better off in respect of comfort. Brick-built accommodation and central heating earned them the title 'The Country Club Set'. One thing, which remained the same irrespective of the building, was the bed, particularly the mattress. Every man slept on three RAF issue mattresses that were known as 'biscuits'– thin cushioned squares inserted into a mattress cover. Unfortunately, this did not stop them from separating when laid upon, often leaving a four-inch gap between each 'biscuit'. Harry Higel, a Special Services Officer, did not remember them fondly:

There was no way you could lay on these mattresses without them separating and giving a draught in the back. We tried sewing blankets around them to

GIs in Nissen Hut with double bunk, Shipdham. *(Al Jones)*

keep them together; we tried sewing the biscuits themselves together, but to no avail.

Harry Slater, a B17 co-pilot, got around this problem when he had cause to visit the quarters of the base doctor. This doctor had a one-piece mattress which he said he had obtained from the base hospital. One day the doctor volunteered to fly in combat with a crew in order to assess the amount of stress experienced by the men. The plane was shot down. Harry quickly exchanged his three-piece mattress for the doctor's mattress and slept in comfort the rest of his time in Britain. He was able to pass the mattress on to his replacement when he was rotated home. Discomfort was further aggravated by the inadequate supply of bedding. One gunner was never issued a pillow and utilised a pilot's foam seat from a crashed aeroplane. The standard issue appears to have been two army blankets, although one desperate ground crew chief took matters into his own hands and admitted stealing blankets. He found himself, one winter, with seven!

Frank Halm was not comfortable in his bed on base: 'At 6' 4" tall, I always had trouble with army beds, seldom could stretch out.'

Clearly, keeping warm in bed was a constant battle against the elements. The area between the springs and 'biscuits' was often lined with insulating material such as newspapers and unworn clothing and a gunner remembered resorting to sleeping in his sheepskin-lined flying gear.

Bert Stiles was a bomber co-pilot, but later in the war became a fighter pilot. Sadly he was killed in action in 1944, but he left a biographical account of his time in England which was published as a book, *Serenade to the Big Bird*. He was based at Bassingbourn in Hertfordshire, and one of the lucky few to occupy an ex-RAF base. Even so, according to the description of his room, he did not exactly live in style:

There were two lockers and a bucket which was used as a waste paper basket . . . There was a pot to put eggs in and boil them on the electric heater, which was shorted most of the time, and which worked pretty well, when it worked, boiling an egg in somewhat less than an hour, Greenwich Time . . . There were two ugly blackout boards in the corner and they looked ugly all day. At night they fitted into the windows and stopped all the light from going out, and all air from coming in.

Rather amazingly, this description was summed up with the words:

We were lucky to live in such a place.

25

It was almost impossible to keep warm in the British weather. The huts were cold and damp and any clothing left around would be covered in mildew quite quickly. Each hut was supplied with a small solid fuel stove of British manufacture, which the GIs called a 'Tortoise Stove' because of its slow heating capacity, but these were later replaced by an American variety which was more efficient. Some men removed the firebricks from the British variety having had no experience of burning coke. The consequence was that the sides of the stove usually melted, although it must have worked in some cases because a gunner remembered his stove thus 'adapted' which would burn all evening, leaving a glow at 2–3 in the morning which nicely coincided with the time they got up for their next mission.

Robert Arbib wrote a lucid description of his experience with the British stove:

> *After supper the first man back to the hut built a fire, if we had any fuel, and put up the blackout screens. Our heating plant for this airy, uninsulated steel shed was one small iron stove. To get the fire going entailed a ritual that involved profanity . . . a half dozen false starts, and a hut full of smoke . . . We were not allowed to keep a fire in the stove during the day when we were all out working. Our coal was strictly rationed, and our hut was always damp and cold when we returned at night.*

One ration of coke lasted about two days; after that, ingenuity prevailed over discomfort and a supplementary fuel supply was sought. Stealing fuel from the base supply became more difficult once the military realised what was going on and posted a guard over it. One young man was caught on the coke heap. When the officer asked him what he was doing, he replied: 'Stealing coal, sir.' Frustration turned to sport in the form of stealing fuel from other huts. A pilot remembered these occasions well:

> *We would plan a night raid, usually on another squadron billet. Two men would go in their hut and engage them in a card game, or telling war stories. A signal would then be given to those outside when all of the target hut were inside at which time they would load their jeep with fuel (coal, wood etc.) acquiring their heat for the night. Some would engage guards in conversation on base coal storage areas whilst cohorts were climbing the high fence and heaving the coal over the fence chunk by chunk.*

Frank Halm remembered being

> *daunted by the fuel shortages and we were cold and uncomfortable as many*

others were. Someone tipped us off about how to get coke when the storage area had been refilled. It was possible to get a small shovel under the gate and get a few coke pieces on it. We knew it was against regulation to do so, but we were cold! Some, I was told, had chopped down the King's trees to burn. We did not. Later, our co-pilot bought a pile of scrap wood from a local sawmill and on delivery he stacked it under his bed. I think we all chipped in money to pay for it. Our barracks were never warm, but less miserable when we got extra fuel. Bed was more comfortable, or being gathered around that miserable stove.

In an effort to obtain some measure of comfort, anything combustible was soon pressed into service. Wood lying around was gathered and burned including dead branches on trees, broken fences, telegraph poles and the boxes which transported bombs. Unfortunately, the availability of wood soon deteriorated and the fence that was just a little bit broken, or the tree that was just a little on the dead side, was converted into heat. One man remembered stealing and burning the doors from unoccupied huts!

Some Yanks had come from areas in the USA where, if you needed fuel, you went out and cut down a tree. This was illegal in England but many trees were lost before an order was given to desist. On one occasion some trees were cut down on land belonging to the King. The Camp Commander was ordered to find the perpetrators and charge them with trespassing, 'but no one knew anything'. The Squadron Commander knew which men were guilty and covered up for them, whilst unofficially issuing a stiff warning.

Other incidents were more blatant as recalled by Jim Lorenz, a B24 co-pilot based at Attlebridge:

One day when the Squadron Commander was out, we cut down a large tree on base, sawed it, chopped it and hid bits under our beds and in drawers. The Squadron Commander wanted to know what happened to that tree later, but no one had any recollection of ever having seen a tree on that spot!

Of course, not all fuel was obtained illicitly. Farmers and woodcutters often did a fair trade in selling wood to Yanks.

British plumbing was also a problem. Few veterans could recall the luxury of a hot bath other than those taken in British homes or at the Red Cross Clubs off base. Hot water supplies were a major concern, because very often there were none. According to a gunner, it was only the officers on his base that were allowed hot showers and these were occasionally raided by enlisted men. Clearly though, these showers did not give total satisfaction; Jim Sheller, wrote home to his wife:

Just had a fine long hot bath in a tub. English showers cannot be regulated, except by the firemen, so invariably you either scald or freeze, hence we all prefer tubs.

Facilities were often spread over a large area and the men often had to brush their teeth in one building, shower in another, and go to yet another to use the toilet. Some were as much as a mile apart and worth a bicycle ride. Officers and EMs alike remembered the frequent wash and shave in cold water, even in the depths of winter. Understandably, some men did not or were not able to keep as clean as they wished. Talcum powder was sometimes used rather liberally, but one case is recorded where a man was literally thrown out of the hut due to serious body odour and not readmitted until he bathed – probably in cold water poor man!

Leroy Nitchke, an armourer, remembered that some men improvised with the 'Whore's Bath', in which a small amount of water was put into their tin hat and heated on the barrack stove. A wash and shave could thus be accomplished with a modicum of comfort.

Personal laundry facilities varied a great deal from base to base. There appears to have been a low level of official laundry facilities available, although the men that did use them found they were not enough. The Stars and Stripes (a daily newspaper for the American military) reported in November 1943 that:

British Board of Trade officials yesterday appealed to dry cleaning establishments in the UK to discontinue acceptance of work from the United States enlisted personnel at the request of the Army authorities . . . Three pieces of dry cleaning monthly and nine pieces of free laundry weekly will continue to be provided to EMs.

Some bases offered a service for washing and the base at Bury St Edmunds certainly used the laundry in that town. Jim McMahon, a gunner, recalled that he used the laundry in his local town often:

Laundry facilities were great. You put dirty clothes in a bag and sent them to the laundry. It was kind of like having a wife – almost!

Even so, it remained a common practice throughout the war. One enlisted man recalled that there was one iron in his squadron which was much in demand, although a colleague who was good at ironing earned extra

GIs USING WASHING MACHINE MADE BY MECHANICS AT ROUGHAM AIR BASE. *(Frank Halm)*

income from some officers who paid him around five shillings to iron their shirts and uniforms.

The most popular way to get clothes clean was to employ a woman in a local village. This system worked well and provided many British women with some extra money. Elsie Bevans, a woman who lived in Suffolk, charged ten shillings and sixpence for a bag of laundry, although she recalled that 'the Yanks always complained that I undercharged.' To offset this, many of them put extras in the laundry bag such as soap, candy and cigarettes, which delighted her. One man had his washing done regularly by a local woman in exchange for a few things he had obtained by mail order from the USA. He remembered that she sewed a blue thread inside his clothes to distinguish them from those belonging to other soldiers.

The men sometimes dry-cleaned their woollen uniforms by using 100% octane aviation gasoline which would then evaporate when the clothing was left around outside in the fresh air for just a few minutes. Of course this was strictly against regulations and therefore a Court Martial offence if caught, as fuel had to be brought over from the USA.

A gunner remembered that his 'cotton underwear was washed in the latrine – by hand!'

POST EXCHANGE AT ROUGHAM AIR BASE. *(Courtesy Norma Slater)*

Although the facilities varied considerably from base to base, one thing that all had in common was the Post Exchange, known as the 'PX' which stocked American products. This gave men the opportunity to purchase familiar goods from home such as gum and candy, and also the more necessary items such as toiletries. Cigarettes could also be purchased from the PX, but like many other items they were rationed. Rationing was calculated by the availability of each item, but sometimes, even with the most careful planning, goods were not available. Veterans agreed that they always took their ration even if they could not use it, because goods could be exchanged for something they did want or given away to friends.

The Post Exchange at the 94th Bomb Group at Rougham was open six days a week from 11 am to 7 pm and the sergeant in charge separated each ration into six. There appears to have been little guidance from the top as to the order of opening and distribution, and the smooth running of these facilities seemed to depend solely on the people who ran them. Some combat men complained that by the time they returned from a mission and had been debriefed, their ration was gone, but the Rougham base kept some supplies back for the fliers until they were able to collect them.

All ranks used the same PX and each man was provided with a ration card. As each ration was used, it was crossed off in pen by a member of the PX staff. The ration card of Jim Lorenz, in January 1945 showed the following allocations:

Every week – Beer, soft drinks, tobacco, candy, gum, cookies, matches.

Every two weeks – Four ounces of peanuts, toilet soap, five razor blades, laundry soap.

Every four weeks – Fruit juice, tooth powder or paste, shaving cream, writing tablet, envelopes or portfolio, pipe cleaners, women's handkerchiefs, deodorant, 2 flashlight batteries, 1 flint and wicks, 1 fluid lighter flame or flameless, 1 writing ink, 1 Vaseline (tin or jar), 2 men's handkerchiefs, 1 clothes hanger, 1 Nescafe, 1 pipe, 1 shoe polish, 1 cleansing tissues, 1 bath towel, 1 face towel.

Clearly there was a problem with tobacco, because on 9th November 1944 the *Stars and Stripes* newspaper noted that 'Beginning Monday, troops in the UK will take a bust in cigarette and cigar rations so that combat men may continue to get their full supply . . . The candy quota for UK personnel will not be cut for the time being.'

There were also strictly regulated sales according to availability. This included items such as watches, fountain pens, mechanical pencils, alarm clocks and compacts.

Of course, the British regarded such items as luxuries and many of these goods ended up as gifts to them, or became part of the ubiquitous bartering system. Leroy Nitchke distinctly remembered an old man of 90 who used to hang around his base on a PX day for handouts.

Enlisted men had the added facility of a Red Cross Aero Club which was an on-base service. These Clubs offered the men a varying range of activities including games of bridge, a small library, coffee and doughnuts and a quiet informal place to write letters home. Some American female staff were brought over by the Red Cross, but much use was also made of British girl volunteers. For the men it was a place to meet their friends and to relax on the base away from their living quarters.

The bases served American food as often as they could, but this took a while to establish. The *Stars and Stripes* in November 1943 stated that

AMERICAN RED CROSS AERO CLUB, SHIPDHAM. *(Al Jones)*

although Americans will be entitled to an accepted European Theatre of Operations ration, it is

> *based upon a minimum of shipping from the US and an absolute elimination of all wastage. It allows the Company Commander certain flexibility, but he is watched to see that he uses this leeway wisely.*

The report maintained that

> *The British ration is a good ration . . . But the average American does not like the high levels of tea, bread, potatoes and mutton, or the limited quantity of coffee and the limited variety of fruits and vegetables.*

The American soldier lived on the British ration for a while, but this was later modified to the so-called 'British-American ration' to include items the US soldier liked and to eliminate those for which he had no particular fondness. Some British foods became a joke among the Americans and one was the much hated brussels sprouts – home grown, nutritious and served up at every opportunity when in season. A notice in one Headquarters Office instructed its pilots: 'If you must make a forced landing, do it in a brussels sprouts patch!'

In 1942 the British shipping situation was critical so the Army suspended shipments of poultry, hot-dogs, sausages, turkey and chicken, but then, apparently, the quartermaster found a way of packing them 'so that the amount of shipping saved is commensurate with that of boneless boxed beef'. Brigadier General Robert M. Littlejohn, the European Theatre of Operations Quartermaster chief, was interviewed by a reporter from the *Stars and Stripes*. He revealed that 'substantial quantities of such items as potatoes, cabbage etc.' were obtained from the British Isles, whilst other rations arrived on British shipping from all parts of the world which was 'more economical for shipping to handle on that basis'.

Most Americans realised that they ate well compared to the British forces and civilians. However, some also recalled the earlier food problems. Earl Rudolph, a bomb disposal officer at the Thurleigh base, near Bedford, recalled his first Thanksgiving in England in 1942:

We expected turkey, but we were served with a 6lb piece of tinned spam with feathers stuck in the sides to represent wings!

By 1943 things appear to have improved as Leroy Kuest noted in his diary the wonderful food served up for a Thanksgiving dinner on his base:

. . . turkey, pork chops, gravy, potatoes, peas, carrots, tomato and lettuce salad, cranberry sauce, ice cream and cherry pie. Everyone ate heartily!

Leroy was generally happy with the regular food he received:

There was always plenty to eat even going back for a second helping, though meat was always limited to one piece of whatever we were having. Always a dessert on a day, cake or pies, canned or fresh fruit when available.

This is a striking contrast with the diet of British civilians at the time and most Americans were only vaguely aware of the severity of rationing that the British had to endure.

Another officer, who arrived early in the war, remembered the British rations:

There was always lots of mutton. Our Mess Hall was in a small hut and there were a couple of separate sittings. Those men from the first sitting, having completed their meal, would leave the Mess Hall and walk down the hill passing the second sitting on the way up. The new arrivals would enquire what was for chow. The answer would invariably be 'Baaaaa,' indicating that it was mutton.

One thing that was greatly missed by the GIs was fresh milk. They were forbidden to drink British milk, as it was not tuberculin tested in Britain.

Powdered milk was always available for coffee and cereal, and was used for milk shakes and later ice cream, which was very popular with the Americans – and the local children when they heard about it.

Powdered eggs were seriously disliked, although a gunner felt the mess hall workers did not have the skills to use them properly, as did the British.

Not surprisingly, a black market of eggs and other goodies flourished in areas where there were American Air Bases. East Anglia was rich in farmland and the Yanks had the ability to pay the high prices. Much trading was done with farmers who were delighted to exchange eggs and such like for otherwise unobtainable items such as shotgun cartridges, cigarettes and canned fruit. Fresh eggs were strictly rationed for the British people, often at less than one per week. The Americans also paid enormously high prices on the black market for other scarcities such as whisky.

Coming from a land of plenty, the average American found it hard to appreciate that food was much valued and not to waste it. They had to be re-educated and it was difficult at times. On one base, the mess sergeant felt so strongly about waste that he put a notice in the mess hall:

Soldier, you can't win the war and get back to mom's table by wasting food. When you go through the chow line today tomorrow and in all the days to come, remember this: There is plenty of bread for you, but not one crumb for the swill man's pigs. There is a little kid – lots of kids – hungry and crying for that bit of crust you are throwing away. When we run short of food – and we do – the stuff you have tossed in the garbage can would help a lot. In these times it is not only a sin to waste food, it is stupidity and treason. When you approach the garbage can, look yourself squarely in the face. How about it soldier? A tip: We are dishing it out sparingly. If you want more, come back with an empty meat can. There is plenty for you, but for the swill man's pigs – phooey!

The buildings on base often covered a large area of land and because of the distance from one place to another some bicycles were issued to officers and crew chiefs. The supply diminished over time and more and more men had to supply their own. Bikes were not only handy for getting around the bases, but they were important too in order to get to the pub or to visit civilian friends.

Fielder Newton, a navigator, recalled:

I believe that every GI on the base had a bike and most of them had a bike as they grew up. However, during the Depression some may not have had one.

The first thing we did when we arrived on base was to buy a used bike for about five pounds.

British people recall that the GIs didn't find it easy to adapt to bike riding in England. It is remembered that they often fell off the bike and landed on their knees. They carried other men on the cross bars and there were often two or three on a bicycle; they found it difficult to remember to cycle on the left hand side of the road.

Fielder gave some thought to the difference between bikes used in Britain and America. He remembered:

We had what was called coaster brakes which were applied by pushing the pedal backwards and this braked the back wheel. We had to remember that your brakes stopped the front wheel which could throw you over the handle bar if you were not careful. Speaking of riding around the base in the dark, I was going to the operations building about midnight. The path went through woods and the only light I had was a flashlight. The light went out and I ran off the path into a bush. I didn't get hurt, shook the flashlight which came on and went on to my destination.

The blackout was an additional hazard to cyclists. One base named the bike 'Hitler's Secret Weapon' because of the many accidents which

GIs WITH THEIR BIKES AT 392ND BOMB GROUP, WENDLING. *(USAF via Martin Bowman)*

occurred while using them. After dark many of these cyclists ended up in the drainage ditches that were a common feature in the East Anglian countryside. Many of them were ridden home from the pub and it is not difficult to imagine the casualties.

Bicycles had been the main mode of transport for British country people for several decades, but even if people were lucky enough own a car, they often used bikes because of the petrol shortage. Thus the popularity of the bike increased.

BICYCLE RECEIPT
1943. (Leroy Kuest)

New bikes could be purchased, but they were in short supply, so most Yanks bought them secondhand, either from civilians or from other men on the base who were returning to the USA. John Appleby wrote in his book *Suffolk Summer* that 'a bicycle is almost a necessity in England'. He managed to purchase a bike for £2 from a civilian after about a month and he recorded that it served him well for two and half months, during which time he rode 2,000 miles.

A receipt for a new bike in 1943 showed a cost of £2 10s 0d, but by 1944 secondhand bikes were selling for £10 or £12, such was the demand. Not surprisingly, thefts were commonplace and a ball-turret gunner admitted that when he needed a bike he stole one from another part of the base. Charles Rankin, a Military Policeman, recalled:

> *To the American GI the bikes were more of a toy. Theft was a problem and some of the men would steal them and take them apart. They would then be put back together again to make them unrecognisable from the original. It was enough of a problem to take up the time of the village policeman and MPs.*

Americans did not always appreciate the importance of the bike to the civilians who needed them to get to work or to do war duty. Army issue bicycles were registered, but even that got out of hand with thefts as it became impossible to keep track of who owned each bike. The base at Rackheath, in a fit of exasperation, called in all army bikes, checking them and returning them to their original owners. Sometimes people inadvertently took the wrong bike in the blackout.

An officer recalled that the thing he missed most was his car. Even though he was provided with a truck, it was for military purposes only and not for social activities. Of course, misuse of trucks was a constant problem. Petrol was rationed, so Army business often merged with social engagements and social arrangements, which as we shall see were not uncommon.

3

Meeting the British People

The first and major duty Hitler has given his propaganda chiefs is to separate
Britain and America and spread distrust between them.

A SHORT GUIDE TO GREAT BRITAIN (1944)

Meeting the British public was usually high on the list of priorities for the American soldier. Although the *Short Guide* had given some details about what to expect, it could do no more than outline the main areas of interaction and the difficulties that might be encountered. As we have already seen, both governments were well aware that clashes between the Americans and the British would be disastrous for morale.

The British Government assumed that their people would find the Americans very different to themselves, so in 1942 the Army Bureau of Current Affairs produced a 14-page booklet entitled *Meet the Americans*. This was not made generally available, but was intended for the use of British officers when preparing discussion groups or giving talks. Thus the British public received little guidance in dealing with these 'friendly invaders'. For almost three years England had been a temporary home to the armies of Commonwealth countries such as Australia and Canada, and later the Free French, Czechs and Poles. However, in the case of the Americans it was their sheer numbers that was the main area of concern. The maintenance of good relationships between the GIs and British civilians was vital.

Social integration between the men of the Army Air Forces and British civilians took place on every level of society. Lady Mayhew, who worked as a volunteer for the British Red Cross, recalled giving tea to officers in her country home in Norfolk. Countless other families gave succour to lonely Americans when they were off base. They helped with directions, explained colloquialisms and pointed them in the direction of shelters during air raids.

The British wanted to befriend their American allies to such an extent that in early 1942 the Women's Voluntary Service was competing with the American Red Cross (ARC) for the honour of setting up welcoming parties at the docks. However, by the summer of that year the more personal offers of hospitality from British families were flooding into the offices of the American Red Cross, but it was too soon. The *History of the American Red Cross* (1950) reported that

> *Comparatively few soldiers were willing to forego the excitement of sight seeing and pleasure seeking in a strange land for the quieter and simpler joys of private hospitality . . . Our greatest problem was to get across to the British people our appreciation of their offer, without actually being able to accept their invitations.*

Eventually, the ARC was able to put together a hospitality programme for visiting British homes and this was well used and appreciated by many lonely or curious Americans. Perhaps the most enduring friendships with the British were the unmanaged and spontaneous variety. One long friendship came about when a GI was walking around a village near to his base and asked a woman if he could take a picture of her garden. She agreed and then invited him into her home and he became a regular visitor for the duration of his time in England.

GIs were often introduced to British families through their girlfriends and it was not uncommon for the American to be accepted into the household as a surrogate son. With the biological son usually away in the Forces, there were many stories of a Yank using the son's bedroom, gown and slippers and being treated in every way as one of the family.

Bob Banta, a gunner, recalled that in 1943 he got to know a family through a 12-year-old girl whose mother did some washing for the men of his bomb group:

> *I would not care to leave the subject of Framlingham Station without speaking of Nancy. Nancy was just one of the many laundry kids that appeared frequently to pick up or deliver our laundry. This practice was most*

prevalent in squadron areas nearer to the outer boundaries of the base.

I stood by my bed one day preparing a bag of clothes for Nancy when I recalled something I had forgotten to do. My exclamation 'Oh, my achin' back!' was one common to the GIs. Immediately a sweet soft voice behind me echoed: 'Does it ache?' I looked back at Nancy to see a look on her face akin to concern. After I laughed and explained its meaning to her, the exchange became sort of a joke between us.

Nancy was twelve. She had an unusually attractive face for one so young with a warm personality to match. She was just the type that made you hope she had an older sister, which she did, but who unfortunately was away in service. One day I came upon Nancy trying to balance entirely too many bags of washing on her bicycle. I helped her carry them home to her mother.

12-YEAR-OLD NANCY SAVAGE CARRYING LAUNDRY HOME FOR HER MOTHER FROM 390TH BOMB GROUP, FRAMLINGHAM. *(Bob Banta)*

Nancy's mother invited Bob to stay for tea and a strong friendship developed which continued throughout their lives.

On another occasion, Al Jones, a bombardier, was riding his bike along a country road looking for strawberries. He met an 11-year-old boy who said his father had some growing on a small patch in their garden:

When we were not flying, I spent many evenings with them. They became very concerned for my safety and that of my crew. When we returned after a mission, if we were not shot up, we would break away from the formation and buzz the farmhouse. They would all run out of the house waving their arms.

AL JONES, BOMBARDIER, 44TH BOMB GROUP, SHIPDHAM. *(USAF)*

40

An NCO working in intelligence got so close to one British family that he confided to his diary:

It's just like having a home away from home. I'm going to hate leaving them when we finally do leave here.

Peter Ardizzi enjoyed visiting a British family and recalled:

I had my mother send me a pair of nylon hosiery at least once a month, including a can of canned fruit. I always took the nylon hosiery and canned fruit to a host family that had invited me to a home cooked meal and an overnight stay in a real bed. They usually also served breakfast in bed. They would not accept money for my stay, but I gave the wife my ration card that we received when going on leave, plus the canned fruit. I also gave the husband a pair of nylon stockings which he appreciated more than money. They could use the ration card to purchase many items and I am sure they enjoyed the canned fruit. The husband I believe sold or bartered the nylons for something they could both use. I never asked him what he would do with the many nylon stockings and canned fruit she sent me.

Fred and Winnie Stiff lived very close to one of the runways at Rougham air base. Many of the GIs visited their home and recalled being made extremely welcome. Veterans also had very fond recollections of Winnie as she would stand outside her house every morning waving at each aeroplane as it took off for a mission. It was very much appreciated that Fred and Winnie showed great concern for the welfare and safety of the combat men who were based at Rougham.

Visiting a British home put a great strain on household rations and Americans were discouraged from eating food supplied by a British family. Tony North, who was a Norfolk teenager in the war, remembered that a ground officer, John Copdock, visited his family quite often and stayed overnight, sleeping in their indoor Morrison shelter. He would cycle from his base to visit Tony's family once a week. John was a 35-year-old married man with two children, so he enjoyed spending time with a family rather than attending dances and nightclubs with his colleagues. He used to bring a duffel bag full of about twelve tins of food and also oranges and some soap. The tins of food were unlabelled, but they had codes stamped on them which identified the food for the mess officers, but not the British people or their American visitors. They opened the tins, not knowing what they would find, but enjoyed whatever it was. Tony said that the tinned food was mostly corned beef and fruit and they were always delighted.

Base Mess Officers were sympathetic to the need to assist British people in their hospitality to Americans. Leroy Kuest often visited the home of his girlfriend Margaret and his diary revealed his appreciation:

LEROY KUEST WITH GIRLFRIEND MARGARET, WHOM HE LATER MARRIED. *(Leroy Kuest)*

> *It sure saves on the pocket book, so I always try to take something along in my duffel bag, like my PX ration. Her dad really loves our Chesterfields and P.A. pipe tobacco. I also try to requisition a roll of toilet paper and some sugar out of the mess hall. They are really short of these articles. Her mother was using old dress patterns for toilet paper, and after I found a straight pin in one sheet, I decided to do something about it.*

To the British it did seem that the GIs were 'over-fed', but it would be more accurate to say that they were better fed. Although British civilians were not hungry, they were bored by interminable spam, potatoes, weak tea and root vegetables. American bases appeared as an 'Aladdin's Cave' with tins of fruit, ice cream and orange juice, all of which must have taken up huge amounts of shipping space. Peter Ardizzi recalled:

> *I was fortunate to have an Argus 35mm camera with me when I shipped out. Technically we were not supposed to have a camera! I slept with it all through the war to prevent it from disappearing! I slept with it even on leave. The 35mm was supplied most of the time by our photo lab on the Base. The film was the beginning and ends of the combat films taken by the aircraft in combat. Our pictures were developed by our lab on the base, or at mail order film processing firms in the States. In all cases they were CENSORED by Government censors and anything they thought had some value to the enemy was removed off the negative. This gave the appearance that you missed a shot on the roll of film.*

Some encounters were brief but nonetheless important, as recalled by Jim McMahon:

> *I had just visited my girl in Luton and was waiting in the cold and rain for a bus. A woman came out of a house and invited me in. Her husband made me sit by the fire while they made me tea and watched for my bus. When the bus came, they both embraced me and wished me luck.*

A more essential 'safety valve' friendship was supplied by British civilians to fliers as recalled by Dick Carboneau, a gunner based at Bassingbourn. After one particularly bad mission where a friend had been killed, he telephoned a British couple he had met only once and asked them if he could spend the night with them. They agreed and he returned to work the next day refreshed. Sometimes, British friends never knew what eventually happened to their American friend who used to visit them.

The *Short Guide* had tried to prepare the GI for the quieter British personality, telling him that he would find the British reserved, rather than unfriendly. Robert S. Raymond, author of *A Yank in the RAF*, wrote home to his parents:

> *The popular conception of the average Englishman as a silent figure behind his 'Times' newspaper in a railway carriage is, in general, a true one. They rarely speak to a stranger unless directly addressed, enter charily into a general conversation unless directly concerned, and are usually unsociable among strangers or when alone in strange surroundings.*

This was difficult for the sociable Americans, but on the other hand *Meet the Americans* warned its British readers that

> *we should expect Americans to be different from us . . . The American soldier's mind is still in civvies even when his body is in uniform . . . They are naturally individualists . . . The dollar is scalp, the symbol of achievement and success . . . They delight in telling tall tales, wordy battles full of cross-talk, wisecracks and jeering remarks which sound, and are meant to sound (but not to be) fantastically offensive.*

Towards the end of the war, Margaret Mead, the American sociologist, wrote an academic booklet entitled *The Yank in Britain*. Mead felt that not enough use had been made of the British home by Yanks because the houses were smaller and did not have central heating. The American therefore had to go to the hub of the family and might feel awkward if, for instance, he did not know how to use a knife and fork correctly. She said that some invitations might have been refused for these reasons.

A letter from Robert S. Raymond, written to his parents, informed them that:

Most of my leisure time is spent answering their questions about the United States. To them it's a country to be described in superlatives, where an ordinary workman can own a motor car, where a telephone is a convenience, not a luxury as it is in England, where ice is used to cool drinking water, where everything is done in a hurry, where education and opportunities for young people are much greater than in England.

Without doubt much civilian interest was directed towards the Americans as Hollywood movies gave them the impression that Americans all had large houses with labour-saving devices, televisions and refrigerators. For many GIs this inflated perception of their social and financial position by the British encouraged the already well established tradition of bragging and this was noted by Appleby:

By some curious coincidence every American soldier sent to England had been making a minimum of 200 dollars a month in civvies street, as he told it, equipped with central heating, electric washing machine and refrigerator.

Arbib, however, did not think that the natives were fooled for long:

For the British it was a shock to find that we did not all swagger like Texas cowboys, that we were not all facially equipped like Hollywood idols, and that we did not speak much like gangsters from Chicago's south side . . . Americans found that there were other groups in Britain besides an arrogant aristocracy, an ignorant, comical class known as 'cockneys' and the ubiquitous English butler.

Many of the British people poked fun at the Americans for being 'over-sexed' and circulated jokes such as 'one Yank and they're off!' (referring, of course, to women's underwear!) and a GI's favourite breakfast being 'a roll in bed with honey!'

The men of the Army Air Forces that did integrate well with the British generally found them to be warm and friendly. However, the cultures were often dissimilar and there were some complaints about the British character and way of life, one of these being the perceived short working hours of the British day. Raymond made a rather arrogant diary note to this effect:

Met a girl (Heather) who works for the Admiralty. Heather works from

44

9.30 until 5.30 which is quite typical of the hours kept by Government workers and civil servants now, in the 3rd year of the war. The truth is that the English have neither the capacity nor the will to work of which my own countrymen are the outstanding example . . . The force of tradition and precedent is so strong that thinking in politics, business, religion etc., seems to have congealed. These are the most economically backward people I have ever encountered. Labour-saving devices and short cut direct business methods are heartily resisted . . . Too much tea drinking, Friday to Monday weekends.

This attitude would certainly not have endeared him to the average British person who, during wartime, was probably doing more than one job anyway. Nearly all office workers undertook voluntary evening work of some kind such as fire watching, although this may not have been obvious to anyone else. The amount of tea consumed by the British was a constant joke among the Americans and many of their base shows produced skits on the British liking for tea. It is unlikely that there is much substance to this criticism because from July 1940 tea was rationed to two ounces per person per week (around one cup of tea per day). A more likely explanation is that people continued to offer what tea they did have to American friends when they visited, thereby giving the impression that it was more plentiful than it actually was. Perhaps a more valid criticism was on the English social structure, the so-called class system. GIs found this particularly repellent, coming as they did from a society where one could move upwards regardless of class or rank. Raymond, once again, was incensed by what he found in England:

I sometimes feel that England does not deserve to win this war. Never have I seen such class distinction drawn and maintained in the face of a desperate effort to maintain a democracy . . . This nation seems inexplicably proud of its defects and its national character . . . these people are provincial and narrow minded, self-indulgent and conservative to a degree unbelievable.

One place where an American could meet the British socially was the pub – always known as 'The Local' to its regular customers; it provided warmth, comfort and friendship for the Americans. Pubs varied considerably in size and atmosphere and were very different from the American bar that was merely a place to go for a drink. Many British pubs had a history spanning hundreds of years and were considered the hub of the local community.

An immediate problem arose concerning the strict rationing of beer which took no account of the pressure of having an American air base nearby. It was not unusual for pubs to be drunk dry by thirsty GIs. Doris Foster, the landlady of a pub in Royston, Hertfordshire, near the base at Bassingbourn, remembered that her supplies came in on Tuesday of each week. Her pub was open on Wednesday, which was market day, and not subject to such strict licensing laws. There would be a few beers left on Thursday morning. The draught beer might last until Friday, then she would have to close until the following Tuesday.

Arbib muses on the fact that during the first week of the Americans' arriving, his local, the Dog, went dry. It was closed for the first time in the 450 years of its history.

The licensing laws were a frustrating annoyance to many Americans. They were irritated and bemused when the landlord called 'time gentlemen please' ten minutes before closing time, which was 10 pm. Of course, laws were occasionally broken and the White Horse at Ashwellthorpe, near Hethel, was fondly remembered by Vernon Ellis, an aeroplane mechanic:

It was actually the home of an elderly couple whom we knew only as Ma and Bill. They both seemed to like us Yanks and occasionally when rations were low they would lock the door and tell the thirsty Britons they were closed, all the while letting us in the back door. That way they would also stay open long after legal closing hours. There would be singing and music far into the night. We would bring a guitar and we always had someone who could play the piano and we would sing and drink for hours . . . Every evening the MPs would make the rounds of all the country pubs to check for uniform violations, passes and other silly things. As soon as Ma heard their jeep coming, she'd lock the door, straighten everyone's necktie, button everyone's blouse and, for those who had too much beer, she'd drag them upstairs or into a closet and only then would she allow the MPs to enter. I'm sure many of us were saved from Court Martial by her kindness.

There was also another pub called 'The Horseshoes' which was run by Sidney and Margie . . . Sidney was asthmatic and not very fond of Yanks but Marjie was buxom, robust and liked beer, Yanks, bawdy jokes and parties. She would always join us while Sidney sulked and wheezed behind the bar. He'd lock the door at closing time and stop selling beer, but Marjie would take over the bar and the party would continue. The last time I recall going there, Sidney suddenly appeared from behind the bar with a double barrelled shotgun.

46

There was an immediate exodus of Yanks and to the best of my knowledge,
none of us ever went back.

For some the local pub became a retreat from the homesickness and drudg-
ery of war and many GIs became regular customers. Tom Forsythe, a Master
Sergeant, had his 'own' chair in front of the fireplace and a bottle of Guin-
ness was always put aside for him. He left his pipe on the mantle and knew it
would be there when he came in the next time. Even the Americans who did
not drink alcohol often appreciated the unique and intimate atmosphere
of the local pub. The pub was a happy place to be where people could relax,
sing, play board games such as draughts (checkers) or play darts. Darts was
a new game to the Americans and they took to it with enthusiasm. Throughout the war, many dartboards disappeared from the pubs and contemporary photographs show that at the same time many boards appeared on hut
doors on American bases! Shove ha'penny was a new game of skill where
halfpenny coins were laid flat and 'shoved' across a board marked out with
lines. The coins had to come to rest between the lines without touching
them.

The GIs were somewhat less enthusiastic about the draught beer which
they complained was warm, sweet and flat. They joked about its diuretic
qualities saying 'Drink one and P38' (a P38 was an American aircraft). British beer was sold at room temperature, although to the Americans, who
were used to refrigerated drinks, it appeared warm. They were unable to
distinguish among the many types of British beers which were all unfamiliar
to them. They mostly drank the bottled, gassy variety, which was the closest
they could get to American beer. 'Bitter' was the drink of the common English man, but few Yanks ever got used to it. 'Mild' was darker and sweeter,
so they often drank the two mixed together, known as 'arf 'n' arf' (half bitter
and half mild.) Although beer was below peacetime strength, the *Short Guide*
warned its readers that 'it can still make a man's tongue wag at both ends',
and Appleby was embarrassed at the derision of a fellow American:

We had a small but vociferous minority who tried to make life pleasant to
our English hosts by getting drunk at their pubs on their beer which the
Americans loudly proclaimed, as they swilled pint after pint, was not fit for
hogs to drink.

Spirits were even more difficult to come by and were closely guarded by
publicans who sometimes kept their rations under the counter to serve to
their most valued customers.

Many publicans did their best to cater for the taste of their American customers by trying to serve the beer as cold as they could. In the winter the bottles would be put outside for a while before serving, but one bar-man went to the trouble of obtaining ice from the local butcher every day, putting it in a tin bath and covering it with a blanket. Into this he put several bottles of beer using them from one end and replacing them at the other. He also recollected that some Yanks put salt in their beer – a very strange thing to the British.

Something which often annoyed local people was the American habit of spreading their loose change on the table before paying for something. This was acceptable practice in the USA, but appeared as ostentatious to the British. Even worse was the occasional flippancy displayed by some GIs. For example, Dan O'Keefe recalled that one evening in 1944 he went to a pub with some of his crew. They jokingly asked the barman how much his stock was worth. He replied that it was worth around £500. The men slapped their wallets on the counter and said jauntily 'We'll take the lot!'

Jim Sheller said he tried to savour the pageantry of all the pubs he could:

An evening would start off quiet and proper, then end up with we Americans playing darts and singing risqué songs, by the old piano. And if some British servicemen were there, we lost in darts and the songs were really risqué.

Pubs were also a great place to buy snacks, although the nature of the available fare depended on the ingenuity of the publican. Doris Foster, a land-lady, remembered that as no meat was allowed to be sold, she made pies by boiling bones and using the stock mixed with potatoes, sage and onion. Partridge and game were not rationed, so in the season she purchased as many as she could from the butcher, cooked them and charged five shil-lings each. They were served at the end of the evening and she recalled it was a good way to get the Yanks out of the pub at closing time because her husband would tell them to eat outside as he did not want grease on his carpet. Then the door was shut.

GIs did not enjoy the idea of meat in a pie, as in the USA they only had experience of pies that contained fruit. Dan O'Keefe bought a pie once and when he took a bite from it and found that the filling was meat, he said it made him 'feel sick'.

One way to satisfy hunger on the way home from the pub, or to round off an evening, was the popular and traditional fish and chips. They were

GI WITH A RABBIT HE HAS JUST SHOT TO EAT. 95TH BOMB GROUP, HORHAM. *(John Bright)*

served hot and steaming, wrapped in newspaper. The fish itself and the fat in which the meal was fried were rationed, so it followed that any fish and chip shop that was located near an American base often ran out of supplies before every customer was satisfied.

Supplementing the regular food which was available on base was turned into a sport by the Army Air Force. All flying crews were issued with a .45 pistol which they kept in their huts. A pilot admitted that they would often take to the field to find an unwary pheasant or rabbit. These would then be cooked on the coke stove in the hut – not perfect, but fun. Earl Rudolph recalled the time when he was game hunting and almost caught by a gamekeeper yelling 'Bloody Yanks!' He said that the gamekeeper was close enough for him to feel the man's breath on the back of his neck. He lost a precious boot in the escape, but managed to get away without being injured.

In Norfolk, two young Americans were court-martialled when they were caught poaching by a landowner and in their panic they had shot and killed him.

Some of the warmest and most enduring memories the GIs have of their time in England concerned the children who were considered to be losing out on a normal childhood. Relationships with children were uncomplicated as their demands were small and easy to satisfy. They did acquire a taste for gum which gave the Yanks no peace thereafter. Shabbily dressed children deprived of toys and sweets and fathers away from home were very common and American hearts went out to them.

It wasn't only the married men who felt strongly about the plight of the children and Arbib felt that this was because the Americans were mostly young men 'and children figured somewhere in their present life or in their dreams'. Bill Anderson recalled that he would sometimes fill his shoulder bag with oranges to distribute amongst any children he encountered. One day a mother ran after him and, with tears of gratitude running down her cheeks told him her that her children had never seen an orange before.

Involvement with children was good for morale. It gave the GIs a great deal of pleasure to share their sweet ration and to throw parties whenever they could. At Christmas collection boxes would be put by the PX asking for donations of candy bars, chewing gum, canned fruit and cookies from the men's weekly rations. Mechanics and carpenters made crude toys from scrap and electricians made Christmas lights by stringing wing-tip lights together. Tony North remembered that on one occasion, on the

Two boys at Hardwick base, 1944. *(Jim McMahon)*

base at Rackheath in Norfolk, a B24 bomber was sent into the air with ice cream mixture in the bomb bay and told to stay up there until the confectionery froze!

The *Stars and Stripes* newspaper noted in December 1944 that 'Last year approximately 7,000 children were guests at American bases throughout the British Isles.' Miss Winifred Rose, who was secretary of the War Orphan Fund, asked the servicemen if they would make Christmas toys for the children.

A medical orderly recalled that British children were welcome on their base in groups or individually:

> There was one boy about 12 years old who visited the hospital area with eggs or whatever. We would give him soap, gum, discarded clothes etc. He seemed eager to be accepted among the GIs and to be one of us. We too were always striving to be accepted by them.

Small boys in particular were often being chased off aircraft by the MPs, but mostly men turned a blind eye to them so long as they behaved themselves. Tom Forsythe recalled the three boys who lived near his base:

They played around the wrecked Fortresses. At first they just watched the mechanics at work, but after a few days they asked for permission to look more closely, then the interior. The visits soon turned into a game with each boy taking turns as pilot, bomb aimer and gunner.

One boy got an even better deal as recalled by Al Jones:

One day I asked Herbie's mother if I could take him for an aeroplane ride. She agreed and after several false starts, I was finally able to schedule his ride. We were to fly our plane to check out the repairs that had been made after one of our missions. I went to the farm and got Herb and took him to the mess hall for breakfast. Now here's a lad of 11 years old, who had never been 15 miles away from home, or ridden in a car. The only motorized vehicle he was ever on was his uncle's motorcycle. I told the crew chief what I was doing and we smuggled Herb aboard. The others picked up parachutes and my flying gear and rode out to our plane in a jeep. I stationed Herb right back of the pilot during take off as I had certain duties to perform during this time. As we went down the runway on take off his eyes got as big as saucers and he hung on for dear life. Once in the air we headed for London while the navigator checked out some of his equipment. We flew over the town and showed Herb the balloons with the cables attached to prevent dive-bombing. We then went up to the bombing practice range on The Wash. I took Herb up in the nose while I dropped a few practice bombs. I then did most of the work on the last bomb and left him to operate the sight for the last few seconds then 'bombs away' . . . We flew up to Scotland and across to the Irish Sea. I took him back into the waist through the bomb bay and to the waist guns. We got down on the ocean and I let him fire the guns into the water, without shooting our tail off of course. We then headed home where we buzzed the farm and he waved to his parents and sisters before going in on our landing.

This was clearly against regulations and the crew knew that they would have been court-martialled if caught.

Tony North was returning home on the train to Norwich from a visit to Ipswich with a friend. He remembered that they shared a carriage with an American officer. During the journey an aeroplane flew overhead and the boys showed a clear interest in this. The American picked up on this and invited the two boys to visit his base at Horsham St Faiths. He sought permission from their parents and then sent a jeep to collect them. He showed them around the base and even took them inside a B17. He provided a lovely meal for them at the mess and they had a great time.

British war orphans received even more special treatment. Quite apart from those in institutions such as Barnardo's Homes, individual orphans could be sponsored by any unit that was able to collect the sum of £100. The sponsoring programme was administered by the ARC and the military newspaper *Stars and Stripes*. This was not a new idea. A similar scheme had operated effectively during World War 1 with French children and this was merely being extended to meet a need in Britain. Orphans would visit the base which had 'adopted' them, collecting gifts of candy or toys, but mostly just revelling in the individual attention from their GI 'uncles'. This positive aspect of 'adopting' an orphan is further outlined in the book *Skyways to Berlin*. The first visit of three-year-old orphan Maureen to meet with her sponsors apparently coincided with a change of luck for the squadron. Every ship came home that day after really tough opposition. This particular squadron had experienced a run of bad luck and, seeking to improve their morale, three non-commissioned officers went to London to look for an orphan to 'adopt'. They took with them £101 which they had collected. The soldiers hoped for a boy, but the Red Cross workers produced golden haired Maureen who, it is recorded, 'went to the soldiers willingly.'

Relationships between the American and British military personnel

SQUADRON ORPHANS, 44TH BOMB GROUP, SHIPDHAM. *(Will Lundy)*

were not so straightforward. The *Short Guide* referred to their opposite number as the 'Tommy' (the British soldier), but of course their opposite number was the Royal Air Force. The bravery of the 'few' during the Battle of Britain had earned them a reputation second to none and they were seen as the heroes of their time by the British public. The high status afforded to these men seems to have been extended to the American fliers who quickly gained the respect of the British community.

The British Army was another matter. They had suffered defeat at Dunkirk and many of them were fighting and dying in the Far East and in Africa when the Yanks arrived. They were a tired fighting force; their food and pay were poor and they had been separated from their loved ones for a long time. Many of them were in no mood for 'invaders', friendly or otherwise, living in their villages, drinking their pubs dry and clearly eating better, being paid more and generally taking everything for granted. The *Short Guide* warned the Americans about possible friction in this direction:

> *Two actions on your part will slow up the friendship – swiping his girl, and not appreciating what his Army has been up against. Yes and rubbing it in that you are better paid than he is.*

It is probable that the expression 'over paid, over fed, over sexed and over here' was coined by a disgruntled British soldier, but the Americans quickly countered this stating that the British soldiers were 'under paid, under fed, under sexed and under Eisenhower'. The RAF came with the highest regard, not only because they were doing the same job, but because they were often thrown together in work situations, or having to land on each others' bases.

British soldiers were always in evidence and the Americans on leave needed a level of sensitivity for situations that might result in trouble if handled carelessly. Unfortunately their youth and inexperience was often against them and a few harsh words could quickly deteriorate into fist fights. Many GIs understood the feelings being experienced by the 'Tommies' and even had some sympathy for them, as noted by Appleby:

> *although there were countless friendships . . ..it is undeniable that the average British soldier rather resented our presence in England . . . By British standards we were pampered . . . Our food was much better than theirs, our pockets were bulging with cigarettes, candy and chewing gum, and we gave the impression that we had more money than we knew what to do with.*

An aeroplane mechanic remembered that on many occasions British soldiers refused cigarettes and drinks offered by GIs because they felt they were being 'bought'. This feeling was understandable, but nonetheless hard on the American who was offering a genuine friendship. Appleby, for instance, was able to establish a close link with the people he met, but as a man in his late thirties, his experience of life would have helped. In his eight months spent in Britain, he proudly noted that he only once spent a social evening with an American. The rest of his leisure time he spent with English soldiers and civilians and he wrote very warmly about those friendships.

The discrepancy in pay scales was brought out into the open in the *Stars and Stripes* in December 1943. It reported that Members of Parliament had demanded the day before that 'in justice to British soldiers, their pay should be boosted to that of American servicemen' (an increase of more than twice as much). Clement Atlee, Churchill's deputy, replied that it was not possible to make comparisons between British and American pay scales.

It did not help that British forces were not welcome in the American Red Cross Clubs unless taken in by an American as a visitor. This was particularly galling because British Servicemen's clubs were open to all military personnel. Food and entertainment were better in the American clubs and what girl wanted to eat a spam sandwich with a cup of weak tea when she could get a burger and fresh orange juice from an American boyfriend? The British soldier could not compete here.

The Americans viewed the British policeman with a mixture of amusement and respect. In rural areas the 'bobby' (so named by the British public after the founder of the Police Force, Sir Robert Peel, who was Prime Minister in the 1830s) rode a bicycle and this, together with his unusual pointed helmet, caused him to be seen as a somewhat comical figure. However, it was soon apparent that he wielded authority and worked closely with the military establishments to keep order.

John Appleby wrote of an experience during one leave when he called into a police station to ask if they could recommend where he could find a room for the night, as all the hotels were full. They invited him to spend the night in a police cell which he accepted and discussed with the duty officer what time he would like to be woken up.

Then I settled down to the most comfortable night's sleep of many months, to be awakened the next morning by a cheery 'Here's a nice hot cup of tea for you sir.'

4

Romancing the Girls

The Young American will find the English girls very interesting and entertaining.

CHARLES W. KERWOOD

The first groups of Army Air Force men to arrive in England in 1942 and early 1943 were delighted to be welcomed by so many young women, but unfortunately for the GIs this happy situation did not last. As more and more units arrived the male to female ratio narrowed and then reversed so that the girls could take their choice from thousands of eager Americans.

Although life before the Americans arrived had not been without its good times, their presence did introduce a lot of colour into the austere, grey lives of British women. To a certain extent they had adapted to life with most of the young men away; they accompanied each other to dances, cinemas and pubs and were mutually supportive through the ups and downs of living in a nation at war. British girls in their teens and twenties had considerable experience of austerity, and the arrival of the men of the USAAF brought a welcome change of pace to their leisure, breaking the in-terminable routine and introducing a host of refreshing social and cultural differences.

The Americans found some of these social and cultural differences enlightening. They had not expected to find so many young women in uniform, but Britain had been at war for almost three years prior to their arrival. The Battle of Britain had been fought and won, and the immediate threat of invasion was over. Many of the girls they saw in uniform were veterans of the war themselves, having manned huge coastal defence guns, been bombed and shot at and proved themselves capable of working alongside men in the defence of their country. Jim McMahon remembered that his bomber crew, when forced to land on a British base soon after arrival, were aghast when a British lorry arrived on the tarmac to take them to the flight line. The lorry was not only driven by a girl, but carried a group of girls who then set to work servicing their aircraft.

A *Short Guide to Great Britain* (Washington, DC: US War Department, 1942) unashamedly tried to instil into the Americans a respect for British womanhood. It stated that soap was so scarce in Britain that

> *girls working in the factories often cannot get the grease off their hands or out of their hair . . . British women have proved themselves in this war. They have stuck to their posts near burning ammunition dumps, delivered messages afoot after their motorcycles have been blasted from under them. They have pulled aviators from burning planes. They have died at the gun posts and as they fell another girl has stepped directly into the position and 'carried on'. There is not a single record in this war of any British woman in uniform service quitting her post or failing in her duty under fire.*

These young men arrived new and fresh to the war, having had no experience of food rationing, air raids or death on a large scale. Hardly any English girls would have met an American before and, not surprisingly, expectations were based on the images portrayed by the Hollywood movies, of handsome young men and dashing heroes.

The GIs' enthusiasm for enjoyment and pleasure was welcome in wartime England. With no obvious end to the war in sight, they presented a picture of carefree abandon and excitement.

British girls had experienced foreign soldiers for some time, but none could match the Yanks for sheer exuberance. Some girls were a little apprehensive about Americans, having heard stories about their alleged promiscuity and wild behaviour, but in many cases a ready and confident smile from him to her was all that was necessary. The GIs oozed confidence and thrilled the girls by referring to them with unfamiliar terms of affection such as 'honey', 'sugar' and 'baby'.

These men were mostly well mannered and well groomed and enjoyed giving girls gifts of what were luxury items such as soap, perfume and cosmetics. Veterans recalled that nylon stockings were highly prized, but were not available at the Post Exchange on base. DuPont, the American company that began nylon production in 1938, was utilised for war work in 1942, so made no nylon stockings again until after the war. This seriously reduced the availability of nylon stockings which were only accessible from old stock. Cynthia Fleet, a British woman who was in a serious relationship with an American officer, never received any nylons from him and none of her friends were given any, although she remembered hearing a story that a few women did acquire some. Women who were in America during the war recollect that nylon stockings were very scarce even in the USA.

The particular smartness of the American uniform bolstered the looks of every man from the Army Air Force. Combat crews wore a neat looking cap, but some of them removed the metal band from inside and sat on the cap several times to make it look less smart. The reason for this was to give the impression that they had flown several missions, so were not new to the job. These deliberately damaged caps were known to them as a 'fifty mission crush.'

Combat crews wore a white metal badge on their chest which made many of them feel very confident towards the girls who admired them so much. The badge was known among the fliers as 'the silver leg spreader'.

Pam Winfield, a British teenager at the time, dated many Americans and admitted to 'falling in love every other day'. Joan Law, who was 18 years old in 1943 and lived in the village of Clavering in Essex, remembered the arrival of the first Americans in this small community.

There was always a dance on Saturday nights. It was a staid affair, but all the villagers would go. Tea and sandwiches were served, but definitely no alcohol. One Saturday about 30 Yanks descended on this village dance, arriving by bicycle and having first visited the village pub. They were noisy, but happy. It must be remembered that no one in this village had ever seen an American before; all were curious, but the older men were downright suspicious. However, the Yanks made themselves at home by dancing with all the women, even the older ones, and flattering them all. All of a sudden a dead place became alive.

Certainly some GIs took advantage of their supposed movie star image and played up to it with tall stories of their homes and possessions, being unable to resist the chance to impress the British, many of whom were perceived to have a much lower standard of living. It seems that generally the Americans treated the British girls with a good deal of respect, and stories of the over-amorous Yank forcing his attention onto an unwilling lady are rare. Clearly though, many admitted that the hopeful outcome of

HUBERT McMILLAN, 392ND BOMB GROUP, WENDLING. *(USAF)*

an evening was to take the girl to bed and many means of persuasion were employed here. One amusing incident was remembered by Joan Law, who dated several Yanks. On one date, the American informed the reluctant girl: 'Honey, I know as many ways of doing it as there are states in the Union, and you don't know what you're missing!'

'Bed' could have meant anything from a haystack to a hotel room, although some hotels apparently requested marriage certificates before allocating double rooms.

Compared to American women of the era, the GIs found British women physically drab. They had not anticipated the shocking results of an increasingly stringent rationing system. They noticed the lack of feminine items such as cosmetics, deodorant, pretty dresses and hosiery, but any criticism soon turned to admiration. Best clothes were a thing of the past, but generally the girls were seen to be uncomplaining and doing their best in difficult circumstances. Harry Slater remembered feeling very upset on finding two British girls sharing a pair of gloves! Quite correctly the *Short Guide* informed the American men that the British considered old clothes to be 'good form'. Hubert McMillan, a B24 pilot, particularly noticed the girls' red cheeks (probably from the climate, he thought) and their red legs, as only a few of them would have enjoyed the luxury of stockings. Unfortunately, the same man noticed the girls had a body odour problem (no doubt from lack of deodorant and inadequate bathing facilities) and also the poor state of their teeth. Several Americans were perturbed to find that the British girls were often fitted with dentures by their mid-twenties, which was not the case in the USA. Dan O'Keefe remembered hearing a myth surrounding the dental problem that many British people had lost their teeth early due to the impure water in England. Unfortunately, many young Americans believed this and consequently feared for their own teeth if they stayed in England too long!

For most young men and women living through the war, the need for love and sex became more urgent. The resulting promiscuity can in part be attributed to the war itself, but also the independence and liberation of the women, the appeal and attraction of the American serviceman and the novelty of his courtship behaviour. It is true that many GIs just wanted to get on with the war, but many tried their best to live up to the image of the 'over-sexed' Yank.

The fact that British girls found the Americans so appealing must have been a constant source of irritation to the British servicemen. However, Philip Cambridge, a veteran RAF gunner, when asked how he had felt towards the Yanks who appeared more glamorous to the English girls, simply said: 'We often felt sorry for them – for the KIND of girl they attracted – she would often be out for all she could get'. Obviously, this is something of a generalisation. Unlike the native men, the average American soldier would have had no prejudices regarding social class and accent, and such distinctions were irrelevant anyway considering the more significant cultural differences between the two nationalities. It seems that the Americans tended to meet informally the more outgoing type of girl, whilst the more restrained females required a formal introduction.

The larger provincial towns attracted the off-duty men from the USAAF who were looking for an evening's entertainment, and although many made their own way, often by bike, the bases themselves usually provided some transport into the local towns by way of a GI truck. The Americans called this the 'Liberty Run' but in Norwich the locals more aptly named it the 'Passion Run' because it soon became clear that the girls were the main attraction in town. Robert Arbib, who wrote about his experiences in Britain at that time, was shocked at the 'easy familiarity' of the girls in one Suffolk town:

> *Was it wartime excitement and the ever present threat of death from the sky that had induced this 'gather ye rosebuds' attitude? Was it relaxation of the parental influence caused by the absence of fathers, by working mothers and the lack of family life? Was it the sudden presence of a crowd of strange and carefree young men in uniform? Or was it all these things that summed up, were the impact of war on this town and inevitably brought with it new and lowered standards?*

It is understandable in these circumstances that morals were more relaxed during the war than in peacetime and there are many instances of girls saying that they were older than they actually were; Arbib noted that some were as young as 14 or 15 but 'they always said they were 18 at least'. For some unaccountable reason, many GIs overestimated the ages of the British girls and a 24-year-old fighter pilot, Bert McDowell, escorted a girl home from a pub one evening convinced she was about aged about 20. They were met by her scowling father who informed Bert that she was only 16. He said: 'Boy, was I glad to get her home safely and to get out of there.'

Harry Slater recalled that they found the English girls little different to those back home although 'they wore less make up and some drew lines along the backs of their legs to represent seams of their non-existent stockings'. To a certain extent, the girls had accepted that wartime stringency dictated rather austere fashions and Arbib remembered his impressions of the girls of Ipswich:

> *They had beautiful flowing hair, they wore tight sweaters and flat-heeled shoes . . . They went unescorted to the dance halls and to the public houses and it was there that we met them . . . Early in the evening it was pairs of girls and pairs of soldiers in the streets, but by nightfall, the pairs were usually then a soldier and a girl . . . And in some doorways there were the dark forms of a boy and girl pressed close together.*

After dark the blackout was in operation and no doubt this assisted many courting couples, although it also made the return trip to the waiting truck somewhat difficult. The evening would often end with couples kissing each other in reluctant goodbyes by the side of the truck and some men missed their transport and had to walk back to the base, or hitch a lift.

The *Stars and Stripes* in December 1944 featured a small article called 'Hash Marks'. It noted that a GI was overheard in the blackout saying 'My girl has a seven-day kiss. It makes one weak!'

As more Americans arrived in Britain it became increasingly difficult for them to find a girlfriend and Leroy Kuest remembered that in Bury St Edmunds in 1944 there were around five GIs to every girl. He preferred to go to the suburbs of London where the competition was not so great and it was here that he met and courted, for two years, his future wife.

By far the most popular places to let off steam in the war were the dancehalls where the war could be 'put on hold' for a while. Dancehalls had been closed at the onset of war in an effort to deter people from congregating in large numbers with the risk of air raids, but they soon re-opened because dances were important for boosting morale. The dancers were generally the younger members of society and consisted of men mostly in uniform and girls both civilian and military. The Americans particularly liked the girls in uniform, and Dan O'Keefe said they nicknamed the ATS (Army Territorial Service) 'American Tail Supply'. In East Anglia the brown working dungarees of the Women's Land Army soon became a familiar sight during the day, although they reverted to civilian clothes when they were not working.

The large provincial towns in East Anglia boasted a dance almost every night. Dancehall managers particularly welcomed the Americans because they wore lighter shoes which did not tear up the floors like the boots of the British and Canadians. (Eventually, they were allowed to wear ordinary shoes when off duty.) Dances were popular before the arrival of the Yanks, but after their arrival, more girls became attracted to dances than ever before. The 'Samson and Hercules' in Norwich (known by the locals as 'The Muscle Palace') was formerly a swimming pool and was exceedingly popular for many on 48-hour passes. Apparently there was little trouble, but if any did occur, it was dealt with efficiently by the American Military Police. Dances were held there six nights a week.

SAMSON & HERCULES, NORWICH, 2010. *(D. Stuart Photography)*

The town of Ipswich used the Co-operative Hall and St Lawrence's Church Hall. The Corn Exchange at Bury St Edmunds served as a dance hall one night a week where, as a GI recalled, 'a band of ladies came on their own'. British girls quickly adopted the American custom of wearing a flower in their hair, although one Yank never got used to the way girls would put a snuffed out cigarette behind their ear while they danced. It was at the dances that the lack of young men was apparent to the Americans as girls were often seen dancing with each other. Dance orchestras consisted of women or older men. It was not unknown for a GI to take over a musical instrument to liven things up a bit, often slipping the owner a small gift. A new phenomenon for the Americans was the 'Ladies Invitation' where a woman could approach a man and ask him to dance with her. This was based on an old idea, but adapted to cope with the shortage of males. Arbib found that he was 'frankly terrified' of this and that 'many a soldier who fancied himself as a Don Juan must have forsworn English dances for ever the first time he found himself, unwillingly, a wall-flower.'

The men from the Army Air Corps brought to Britain new dances such as 'Trucking', 'Pecking' and the 'Big-Apple', and taught them to the British girls. The best and most fondly remembered dance was the 'Jitterbug' which soon swept across Britain, much to the disapproval of the older generation. The basic steps were simple, but allowed for much freedom of expression as well as the revealing of women's legs and underwear. Pam Winfield who was a teenager in the war, later to become a GI bride, remembered getting ready to attend a dance on an American Air Base. Pam recalled that she and her friend practised swirling in their homemade pleated skirts to find out 'how much we needed to do to show just a hint of knickers'. When dancing the Jitterbug bodily contact was minimal, but the movements were uninhibited. Jitterbug contests sprang up everywhere. The Americans in turn learned the traditional English 'Okey Cokey' which they loved because it was so simple, and they also enjoyed more sedate dances such as the valeta, the Chestnut Tree and the Boston Two Step.

Tea dances were designed to allow people to return home before dark, and were held in the late afternoon, the traditional tea time for the British. However, as the young were mostly working in the day and the evening was the accepted time for romance, these dances were more popular with older people. Pubs closed after lunch and tea dances served no alcohol. Some GIs attended tea dances, if they were available at that time of day.

The American bases themselves also served as venues for dances; some on a regular monthly basis, but more so at festive times such as Thanksgiving, Christmas and New Year. There were also countless other celebrations within the bases, mostly in acknowledgement of the number of missions undertaken by the group. With a celebration for the completion of every hundred missions for a Bomb Group, a party could be held every few months – very healthy for morale. It is understandable that few British girls would wish to be left out of such an occasion, attracted by the promise of American food, as well as lots of attractive young men.

Some parties were well organised with women having to officially request an invitation in advance, whilst others were last minute affairs. One Bomb Group had to send out trucks to find girls for their dances and then discovered they had picked up girls of easy virtue who had not been difficult to find and were much more available. Judith Rabsey, a Norfolk woman, remembered that Christmas dances on American air bases were always popular and girls had to make their request at the Lord Mayor's Office to be vetted and await an invitation. There was always lots of food and alcohol. Girls were picked up by GI trucks and returned to a safe place at the end of the evening. Most events usually wound up around midnight, but there was often a joker who put up a notice stating that 'all girls should be off base in 48 hours'. It seems that some did not make it and a pilot recalled several occasions when he entered his hut after such an evening.

There would be a scramble of bodies and GI pants would rush away, although the rear ends in them did not belong to the men! These girls were often of the 'professional' variety, taking the opportunity to stay on and make some money.

Dances were usually held in a hangar and one man remembered sweeping the floor and putting down soap-powder to make it slippery. Christmas or party decorations would be made from such items as 'chaff' (strips of aluminium foil officially used to drop from the air to confuse enemy radar), popcorn threaded on cotton, and aircraft wing lights. Almost every base at some time would have had the honour of dancing to the famous Glen Miller Band, whose contribution towards morale was well remembered. Although the Band was only in the UK for a total of six months before Miller's disappearance over the English Channel on his way to France, the impact of his music inspired a generation and continued after the war. Anyone who danced remembered dancing to his famous swing music, or the softer themes of tunes such as 'Moonlight Serenade' where a soldier who had a girl could hold her close. Officers and Enlisted Men's dances were held

GLEN MILLER ORCHESTRA AT 94TH BOMB GROUP'S 200TH MISSION PARTY.
GLEN MILLER WAS MISSING BY THIS TIME, SO THE ORCHESTRA WAS CONDUCTED
BY RAY MCKINLEY. *(Frank Halm)*

separately, although it was the EM's dances which were often the more
interesting. For example the 94th Bomb Group at Rougham held a 200th
Mission Party in September 1944. The Enlisted Men's dance was held in
the hangar with the Glen Miller Orchestra providing the music, whilst the
officers used the Theatre building (probably a large Nissen hut) making
do with the USAAF band. There were even occasions when an officer would
borrow an Enlisted Man's uniform to gain admittance to the more exciting
event.

Leroy Kuest remembered the 200th Mission Party on his base:

*Glen Miller's band showed up with Dinah Shore. Glen Miller had already
been lost, but there was no mention of it. Ray McKinley led the band. They
had bought land army girls wafs, civilians, wacs and we danced in the main
hanger on the concrete floor. They served beer, coffee and hot dogs. We had
a wonderful time.*

Elmer Bendiner, a flying officer, reflected in his book *A Fall of Fortresses* on his acquaintance with a lady at an officers' dance at his base:

She was one of a group of girls shipped up in a GI truck like a load of powdered eggs. They were all proper girls from proper homes. They were to be used for dancing and to be held vertically for light love only.

Because finding the right kind of girls for base dances was a problem, Women's Land Army hostels and Nurses' Homes were considered to have great potential and they were approached early on by the dance organisers. These girls were also inundated with requests from individuals, but even if a man arrived with his own partner, a ground crew man recalled 'someone would always cut in'. Gilbert Howard, a British Ministry of Works employee in Norfolk, remembered visiting a Women's Land Army Hostel and finding the warden furious three days after the event, because the girls were still suffering from their over-indulgence in alcohol.

New combat crews were arriving continually whilst the surviving crews were being rotated home on the completion of their missions. With a stay of anything from a few weeks to a few months, fliers had less time in which to establish a permanent relationship with girls than the ground crews. Bearing in mind that the ground staff were in England for the duration of the war, it follows that they had more time and incentive to find a permanent girlfriend. Tom Forsythe remembered that the English girls were considered by some to be one-man girls – 'one man tonight and one man tomorrow!' In 1944 Jim Sheller wrote in his diary: 'Saturday night was dance night on base. Lots and lots of men, very few girls who seem to be occupied by permanent personnel.'

Some girls occasionally did stay overnight on a fairly regular basis, although obviously this was not condoned as it posed a breach of security and the necessary amount of privacy was difficult to come by. However, this could be more easily achieved by higher-ranking ground officers, or people with access to buildings other than their own huts. Jim McMahon remembered that one line chief had a girlfriend who would spend the occasional night with him in the engineering office to which he had a key. This was observed by some of the men and caused concern because she could have been a spy. On this theme Elmer Bendiner recalled that some of the girls, 'with rumpled hair and heavy lidded lustrous morning eyes, would kiss the boys goodbye before a mission. It was not good for security, but it was pleasant for morale.' Girls were sometimes smuggled onto the base in the returning Liberty Truck which rarely received more than a cursory inspection from the Military Police on duty. It appears that the difficulty was in getting the girls off the base. James Bunch, a Technical Sergeant, recalled that on one occasion two gunners who shared a tent were caught by the MPs seeing their girlfriends on the bus early one morning, clearly having spent the night with them on base. The men were court-martialled, but the chaplain on that base requested a transfer in protest because he felt that this was going on all the time and that these men were no more guilty than many others.

However, some women were pursued with a determination which is understandable given the circumstances. Elmer Bendiner, as a flier, recalled that sex was often used as a palliative, but also agreed that 'war did not allow for sustained emotions'. It therefore followed that if satisfaction from a relationship could be telescoped into one evening, it often was. Dick Carboneau, a very young gunner who admitted to having been in constant fear of his life, recalled:

> There was an immediacy, an urgency to life. That was part of the reason some of us could romance the English girls, perhaps even make them pregnant, and not be conscience stricken over it. Viewed in the broader sense, these feelings were quite basic in the nature of man, when threatened with imminent death, and one of the strongest natural drives is to procreate; it's like the law of nature. And we Yanks were pretty law-abiding, I must say.

Some fliers tried their best to get a steady relationship if only for the comfort of having someone to return to in the evenings and to have someone special to care about their safety. However, many admitted that they were happy with a different girl every night, as they were more preoccupied with staying alive than investing in a long-term relationship. Dick Carboneau admitted that his ultimate ambition on a date was to go to bed with the girl, but he never quite knew how to get started. He entertained such ideas with a British girl he dated a few times, but 'was quite fond of her and afraid of offending her'.

> She was in the highly respected Women's Auxiliary of the Royal Air Force, stationed not far from us at Henlow. We dated several times. Each time she wished me luck on my next 'op' as she called missions, and there was always a sound of relief in her voice the next time I called to ask her out. I believe Jean sweated out my missions with me. She didn't want to get serious however. Her fiancé, an RAF pilot, had been killed in action, shot down over the channel and I believe she wasn't ready to be hurt again.

Clearly the importance in maintaining the stability of this relationship out-weighed the thought of immediate sexual satisfaction, even though Dick believed his chances of survival were almost nil.

Jim McMahon, a young gunner, felt that companionship was more important than sex and he never spoke of the future with his English girl-friend:

> I never promised her anything. To me she was someone to unburden my stress upon, having returned from a combat session. Jack (my buddy) was older and more mature than I and had different reasons for dating. His interest was strictly sex. I talked to his girl several times and he was feeding her a line. I never told any girl in England that I would take her back to the great USA, but in my outfit I knew of only one mentioned. Tom, another member of my crew, had a woman in Norwich and spent all leaves with her. She was married to an English serviceman. Tom was also married. In the brief references he made to this, he denied any sexual activity. The other enlisted men in my crew had one-night stands only. One was married, but took what he could get. He made no promise to any girl – just get it and forget it. He was the oldest enlisted man at age 25.

Some of the girls themselves did not want to become too involved with combat men. Such a relationship would have been romantic in a sense, with the kudos and prestige, and indeed one woman referred to them as 'gladi-ators'. These tenuous relationships though brought much worry and fear for the girl concerned. Some girls believed that a flier's life was not his own and that it belonged to the US Army Air Forces and America and could be called in any time leaving the girl high and dry and maybe even pregnant. In an unmarried relationship, she had no status with the US government. She would have no rights to be told of his death or capture and may not even have known unless a friend of his took it upon himself to break the news. For this reason, some women's lives revolved around the missions, listening to the take-off and awaiting the return. They then awaited the telephone call or visit by the Yank, when the panic would be over until the next mission.

Groups of prostitutes known as 'camp followers' were not uncommon around the bases. Tony North remembered that two women in a small Nor-folk village were nicknamed 'The Liberators' for their 'services' to the men from the local air base. In an effort to give the off-duty GI a respectable place to stay, the Bishop's Palace in Norwich was requisitioned for use as a hostel, but the rule was definitely 'No women in the rooms.' Not to be beaten by the system, some servicemen would sign in to be allocated a room, and then climb out of the window with a blanket and pillow to spend the night on the grass below with their girl. One assumes this was summer months only! Doris Foster remembered that Parker's Piece (a flat green public area about a quarter of a mile square) in Cambridge was like an assault course after blackout. One had to step over the pairs of bodies lying on the grass – the women all British and the men's uniforms mostly American.

Even though both nations shared a common language, misunderstandings were rife. A gunner took his British girlfriend to see his B17 which the crew had named FRENESI after a popular song of the time. She stormed off after announcing that she was not going out with someone who thought that English girls were 'free and easy'. Norman Longmate in his book *The GIs* tells the story of a pilot who had spent a weekend with an RAF friend. On his return to the barracks he told his co-pilot that he had just had a marvellous weekend on the Norfolk Broads (a series of inland waterways). The co-pilot requested the name of just one of them because he was going on pass next week!

A cashier in a British restaurant was sitting with a cat on her lap when a group of Yanks were leaving. She innocently asked them what they thought of her 'pussy'. Had she said 'pussy cat', all would have been clear at the time and the resulting sniggers would have been avoided. The word 'pussy' had no sexual connotation in England at that time.

Confusions also arose from the casual attitude of the Americans to the dating of British girls. Dating was common practice in the USA where it had no connotations of commitment, but a fair amount of wisecracking, flirting and petting. However, it seems that the British girls had no experience of this and took the GIs too seriously, often misinterpreting their friendliness as formal courtship. Margaret Mead wrote that the Americans used terms of endearment too easily and were too quick to take a girl's arm. This could be considered as an engagement, or at the very least a serious commitment, and many British girls were swept off their feet with the apparently amorous advances of the Americans, only to end up disappointed.

Geoffrey Gorer, a British writer who worked with American sociologists throughout the 1940s, wrote in his book *The Americans* that 'dating was using the language and gestures of courtship and lovemaking without implying the reality of either,' but that there is no confusion 'when both partners are American'. He further noted that 'dating is idiosyncratic to Americans, but they are unaware of this' and that although dating may be seen as an attempt at seduction, parrying is important and an early victory gives little

Pin Up Entertainment, Hardwick. *(USAF)*

satisfaction. 'An easy lay is not a good date.' It is hardly surprising that a fair proportion of British girls found the whole process of American-style dating and courtship highly confusing.

Aeroplanes were often named after a crew member's wife or girlfriend, or failing that, a fictitious, sexy character such as 'Virgin's Delight', 'Madam Shoo Shoo' or 'Lucky Lady'. The name was usually accompanied by a painting on the nose of the aeroplane of a scantily clad and buxom female figure, often in a seductive position. Pin-ups were very popular both in the workshops and in the barracks and Gorer says that they were openly encouraged by the War Department and seconded by the press so that they would be the last thing a man's eyes rested on before he went to sleep and the first thing he saw in the morning. This, he says, was due to 'the Government's paranoia with incipient homosexuality and the wish to encourage healthy heterosexual interests'. This encouragement of 'healthy interests', plus the normal desires of young men away from home, unfortunately led to an epidemic of venereal disease.

In an effort to control VD, the Army Air Force supplied men with prophylactics (condoms). On a Suffolk base, a ground sergeant informed the troops that 'we've got thirty thousand rubbers (condoms) in the supply room and you people need to do something about this'. This policy proved something of a double-edged sword as it also encouraged promiscuity.

Although promiscuity was not officially condoned, it was difficult, or even impossible, for those in authority to turn a blind eye completely. Dick Carboneau remembered that his base at Bassingbourn held an 'Open Post' in 1944 for civilian visitors and because the Commander knew that the visitors would be mostly girls, he felt it necessary to gather the troops to tell them 'not to behave like a bunch of striped assed apes'. He set a deadline of midnight for all visitors to be off the base because 'anything you haven't got by then, you aren't going to get anyhow'.

According to Longmate, a guide was issued by the Provost Marshall in April 1943 entitled *How to Stay Out of Trouble*. It warned against females of questionable character, but he pointed out that these were, of course, the very women which many Yanks were seeking! Indeed, Harry Slater, who wrote the 94th Bomb Group history, recorded a notice on the group bulletin board which read:

> *The following establishments are off limits to all personnel: Kings Head and the Ma' Café, Loate, Watford and Mrs Ethel May Horne residence, Old Woston Road, Winwick, Huntingdonshire.*

Groups of men were observed making careful notes of the details.

The blackout in Britain provided a haven for prostitutes touting for customers, particularly in Piccadilly, London, where the GIs knew them as the 'Piccadilly Commandos'. Prostitutes could be found anywhere in England, but were more obvious in the large towns, or cities such as Ipswich or Norwich (where they were known as the 'Norwich Nightfighters'). These women all operated illegally, but with the assistance of the blackout, plus the fact that the police were very busy, a fair amount of business was transacted nevertheless. A gunner recalled that he could always pick up a girl in a pub if he wanted intimacy. The opener was a 'lemon gin' (probably gin and bitter lemon). He said he never sought out prostitutes, but some girls would ask for money afterwards. He gave it to them, because he thought 'maybe they did need it'.

For the married man who intended to remain faithful to his wife back home, important female company was sometimes achieved on a platonic basis, although obviously this was difficult and a certain amount of infidelity resulted from the long and stressful separations. For instance, a fighter pilot admitted to having some weekends in London with an American nurse whilst his wife was at home pregnant with their second child. The nurse had recently become widowed after her husband was killed in France and this new relationship sprang up out of sympathy for her by the airman. However, many Yanks did appear to manage platonic relationships with women who were married themselves and merely sought companionship whilst their husbands were away.

Tom Forsythe, a married ground crew man, remembered a woman he met during the war in an English pub. She was also married, but took him home to her parents' house where he was treated like a son and became a firm friend of the family. When on leave, he stayed at the house and regularly accompanied the woman to the cinema and pubs.

Some letters home reflect the loneliness and isolation felt by many married men and one letter written by Jim Sheller to his wife finishes: 'the one thing I do want to do I can't because you're not here'. The writer of this letter was an officer and when on censor duty one day he remembered a letter written by an enlisted man to his wife: 'Honey, take a good long look at the furniture, because when I get home all you're going to see is the ceiling.' Similar sentiments were also found in letters home from GIs in World War 1.

Parental disapproval menaced many a friendship. Understandably, some parents feared for the safety of their daughter's reputation, bearing in mind the reputation of the Americans themselves. Moreover, pregnancy was a real risk and men in a foreign army might not face up to their responsibilities. Quite apart from these hazards, many parents felt that the risk of losing their daughter to an American was just too great and so they openly discouraged, or even forbade, such liaisons. America seemed a long way off in the 1940s and perhaps some parents felt that they would be saying goodbye for ever to their daughter and be deprived of any future grandchildren. Jim Johnson, a Technical Sergeant, felt it necessary to confide to his diary in 1945:

By this time I find myself engaged to a lovely English girl with a typical English first name, Joan. Her folks don't know that we are engaged and that we plan to be married for we have found out that they would never allow this. Since we are not yet ready to be married, we keep it from them. If they did know of our proposal, there would be no end of arguments and unpleasant scenes for her. This plan may be a bit unethical but so seem their reasons for not allowing our marriage . . . It seems to be social differences. They seem to feel superior to us Americans in some way. Joan is not like this and certainly

JIM JOHNSON WITH HIS GIRLFRIEND JOAN IN 1944. *(Jim Johnson)*

shows herself to be different when she is willing to give up her folks, home and friends to go into something as new as the United States, and when she is willing into the insecurity that I have to offer her. We both know that a marriage between two different nationals, even at its best, is not good. But we also know that there is something stronger than tradition and social standings. If ever I loved anyone, she is Joan.

This couple did marry and lived happily together in the UK.

The girls of Britain had a huge experience of war long before the arrival of the GIs, although they coped with the trauma in their own particular way. Jim McMahon was called upon to provide an unexpected support for a British girl he met at a dance. She told him she would like to show him something that would entail a taxi ride. He was curious, so they climbed into a taxi and drove through London. Their destination was a park in the London area and although it was late at night, she indicated to him to sit down on a bench and pointed to a row of bomb damaged houses through the trees and to where one house lay in ruins. She told him that this had been her home and her parents had been killed by the bombing. Jim said he was rather shocked at this revelation, but more so when she collapsed in tears on his shoulder as he had only known her for a few hours and she was now sharing with him her innermost emotions. He was disturbed and unprepared for this experience, although highly sympathetic.

Among the many romantic disappointments and broken hearts of the Americans and the British girls, there were also many genuine love stories – a large number of which have resulted in long and happy marriages. Chuck Galian, who married his British girlfriend and took her to Milwaukee, humorously reflected in the 1980s his first meeting with his future wife in England: 'Our hands met over my wallet.' His wedding was planned to take place in a London church near to his girlfriend's home in July 1944, but for security reasons and just prior to D-Day, Americans were not allowed into central London. Not to be beaten, he rode to the outskirts of London and then took a bus into town riding on the top deck hunched up so that he should not be spotted by the MPs. He not only got to the wedding, but many of his friends from the base were also there.

McCauley Clark, a non-combat pilot whose job involved testing and delivering repaired aircraft, remembered helping out his friend Scottie in an unusual way. They were both posted from England to France just after D-Day and Scottie was loath to leave his girlfriend in England. McCauley was regularly making business flights across the channel at around weekly intervals and would carry messages from one to the other. One day the girl said that she had a very special message for Scottie: 'Tell him I'm pregnant.' Scottie was delighted at this news and wanted to get married right away, but could not get back to England. McCauley, who had a P51 (a Mustang fighter aircraft) which he had adapted to hold two people, offered to arrange the wedding in England, pick up Scottie (who would go AWOL) in his aeroplane and take him to England. The bride and groom would be put into a jeep and driven to their wedding, then he would do the whole process in reverse – all in one day. It was a great success and no one ever knew except the immediate participants.

Some women backed out of marriage arrangements at the last minute, whereas others were very happy and eager to begin their long journey to their new home. In 1945 *Good Housekeeping* magazine produced a booklet entitled *A Bride's Guide to the USA*. It told of the country itself and its people and customs. Most useful of all was the necessary and helpful information it contained for the journey. These journeys were well covered by the American and British press and newsreels in response to the keen public interest in war brides.

Fortunately, the majority of these marriages survived. There was a general upward trend in the divorce figures after the war anyway, but it is believed there was no more divorce among Anglo-American marriages than any other. Marriages made in haste and under the pressure of war were bound to show a peak in divorce rates once emotions were more settled and the future more secure. Stories abound of brides finding themselves deserted on their arrival in the USA, or finding that their husbands had misled them as to what was in store for them. Many were also disappointed to find that the USA was not the paradise they had expected, but far the most common experience for the British bride was good old-fashioned homesickness and for some, the only cure was to return to the UK, with or without their husband.

When a GI wanted to marry a British girl, he had to obtain permission from his Commanding Officer at least two months in advance and marriage did not automatically make the bride an American citizen. She had to apply for naturalisation separately. The couple also often had to undergo a rigorous interview with the base chaplain who felt duty bound to try to talk them both out of it. This usually failed to break the relationship, but after that a mountain of forms awaited the pair.

One unfortunate legacy from the Yanks' stay in Britain was the large number of wartime babies. Pregnancy for the unmarried was not looked upon kindly at that time. It was not only considered shameful, but could be used to opt out of war work, or to trap an unwary GI into marriage and the promise of a new life in the USA. Fortunately, there were not many women who were this unscrupulous. British women certainly felt that the USAAF had little sympathy for their plight and that may have assisted some men to avoid their responsibilities. Some men were deliberately elusive, but there are many stories about women having lost contact with the man prior to knowing about the pregnancy, or more sadly the death of the man before marriage could take place. Events moved fast during the War and relationships took place over weeks, when in peacetime it might have taken months or years. Once a GI had left Britain, there was no way for the girl to contact him, or to know that he was safe, so a girl had to depend on him to continue with the relationship.

In a war zone with little time away from work in which to socialise, opportunities for love and emotional comfort were often snatched whenever and wherever they could be found. Declarations of love made in the heat of war often proved unsustainable, yet many of the participants knew this and readily accepted whatever fate had in store for them.

5

Leisure and Pleasure in the Towns

I stood outside a moment and listened to the City. London under the moon.

Tomorrow it might be Berlin under the sun.

Somehow I didn't care. Everything was different now. For a while I'd been away from it.

BERT STILES, 'SERENADE TO THE BIG BIRD'

For the men of the Army Air Corps, the need to get away from the base from time to time was strong. Although American air bases in Britain contained most material necessities, they were first and foremost military installations operating in a war zone. As such they lacked the warmth and comforts found in a home, but moreover they actively repressed the soldiers' individuality. Many jobs on base were repetitive; with little relief from this monotony, men greatly looked forward to any passes they could receive that would take them off base.

Short-term passes, known as 'Class B', lasted for an evening or a day and were usually spent in the local pub or visiting local English friends. In the long summer evenings when the daylight lasted until 10 pm, the countryside could be explored on foot or by bicycle. Wherever possible, the military authorities utilised the ancient English hedgerows as a boundary between themselves and the English community, although it was almost impossible to maintain tight security with such a system and any airman lucky enough to discover a gap in the hedge effectively

CLASS B PASS. *(Jim Johnson)*

won himself an extra 'short term pass' to the pub, or maybe to visit a girlfriend.

The Class B Pass noted that it 'entitles the holder, whose signature appears below, to the privileges stated on the reverse side' and the reverse side stated:

> *This pass authorises the soldier to whom issued to be absent from billet when not on duty or due for duty except between 0100 hours and 0600 hours on any day, and to visit any place within the geographical limits of . . .* [particular cities and towns were specified].

> *This pass must be used together with some proper means of identification, i.e. WD AGO Form 65, WD AGO Form 65-4, WD AGO Form 65-10 or enlisted man's yellow identification card and identification tags.*

The longer-term passes of seven days were known as 'furloughs'. These gave the men time to really get away, to eat or even sleep out, and to travel further afield. These passes were precious and although officially they were supposed to be granted every 21 days, in reality they were issued far less often. Leroy Kuest remembered that they received two 48 hour passes each month and after a year, a 7 day furlough was issued. He received two of the latter during his time in the UK and spent both in Scotland. He recalled that travelling to London from his base near Bury St Edmunds was not an easy journey as

> *train travel was not that good. At first we rode the train, but it took mostly half a day. We called them milk trains because they stopped at every village. Later we hitch hiked, catching mostly trucks as there were very few cars on the road. We would hold up a packet of cigarettes. If they stopped and were going to London, they would get the whole pack. Otherwise if only going a short way, we would pull out two cigarettes and bid them goodbye for stopping. The word soon got among the truckers, so they always stopped.*

LEROY KUEST ON LEAVE IN SCOTLAND. *(Leroy Kuest)*

The provincial towns of East Anglia had much to offer the GI on pass. Robert Arbib wrote:

> *They wanted relaxation, they wanted release, they wanted a change from the gruelling drudgery of the job . . . the towns served merely for an escape, a blowing off of steam, a release from confinement, and they were the only diversion that the world could offer us at the time.*

Norwich, the county town of Norfolk, was very popular and local people recalled that the streets were always lined with Yanks. For those with an interest in history, it boasted a 12th-century cathedral and the remains of a medieval town wall. However, the City of Norwich also catered for the more popular recreational needs such as dancing, eating and drinking.

The American Red Cross (ARC) provided accommodation for the US serviceman off duty. The Palace of the Bishop of Norwich was requisitioned for the use of EMs and the Bethel Hospital for officers. The Bethel had formerly been a mental hospital and those American guests, visiting before

THE BETHEL, NORWICH, 2010. *(D. Stuart Photography)*

the refurbishment had been completed, recalled sleeping in padded cells.

Although these facilities were operated by a nucleus of American personnel, they also provided employment to many British civilians and took advantage of local people who wished to volunteer their services. In the Bishop's garden, a purpose-built dormitory was erected to sleep 5,600 men in two- and three-tiered bunks. Gilbert Howard, who was an Inspector for the Ministry of Works, said there was a small kitchen for the use of guests, where they could make sandwiches and coffee.

The Bethel became a home from home for one officer crew and they slept there as often as they could. When free, they would spend the day in Norwich and call into the base later to see if they were on alert for a mission the next day.

BETTY WARD, RED CROSS WORKER AT THE BETHEL, NORWICH. *(Jim McMahon)*

If not, the trip was extended into the evening and overnight at the Bethel where they were comfortable and could make themselves at home.

A wartime report on the Norwich Clubs by Mrs Helen Johnson, club director, showed that activities available in the November of 1944 included football, basketball, and a ping-pong tournament, as well as fencing lessons which were 'immensely popular'. Another favourite event was the late evening 'kitchen party' at the Bethel where corn was popped and 'fudge or toffee made.' The highlight of this particular month was, of course, Thanksgiving and Mrs Johnson stated that 'there was cider with the dinner and coffee in the lounge afterwards'.

Cambridge was popular for some, but did not suit all tastes. Jim Sheller wrote in his diary: 'A quiet restful spot, if a bit dull.' Conversely, John Appleby was

dazzled by the beauty of the place . . . if there is anything this side of heaven more beautiful than Cambridge, as seen from The Backs on a sunny spring or summer day, I just don't want to see it. Cambridge will do for me.

Cambridge, too, had an American Red Cross Club at the requisitioned Bull Hotel and some veterans remembered the Eagle pub in town where Allied servicemen wrote their names on the ceiling with a lighted candle. The ceiling remains there today, with all the wartime inscriptions preserved. The Dorothy Café was also popular, and it is recorded that 'the hall was filled with smoke, small tables, a local band, subdued lighting and a small wooden dance floor'. The Dorothy Café did not last long after the war and by the 1970s had become a furniture store.

Of course the colleges and historic buildings gave pleasure to many visitors, but the general mood was one of quiet dignity rather than a place for a wild night out.

For the more serious minded, the ancient and famous colleges had to be seen to be believed and Jim McMahon remembered that one day he and a friend decided to look more closely at one of the colleges. They entered through a large oak door and found themselves in a corridor. Soon, an elderly man appeared and enquired as to the reason for their visit. They replied truthfully that they just wished to look around. Without any hesitation, the man asked them to follow him where he showed them to another huge oak door indicating that they should go. They were surprised to find themselves on the 'outside of the combine'. Hardly a word had been exchanged, but the meaning was clear.

THE EAGLE PUB, CAMBRIDGE, 2009, WITH ORIGINAL WARTIME GRAFFITI ON THE CEILING. *(D. Stuart Photography)*

Another rather amusing incident occurred in the town of Colchester and involved a fighter pilot who spent the night in a hotel with girl. In the morning, the hotelier asked if the young lady had stayed the night. The couple looked a little uncomfortable and the girl blushed, but the pilot said that yes, she had indeed stayed all night. The pair, expecting to be subjected to a moral lecture, were much amused when the hotelier then stated: 'In that case, the lady must sign the register.'

Few GIs based in Britain during the war returned to the USA without first visiting London which was the Mecca for servicemen of all nations. Americans were attracted there for a variety of reasons. Some went for the history, the theatres and museums, but most went for the pubs, the dances and the girls.

For many men from the Army Air Corps their first two- or three-day pass was spent visiting London, and many admit they went there at every opportunity. A city of fame and infamy and the subject of many American cinema newsreels, it was often the place in England that the Yanks were most keen to explore. However, London was also a place of anonymity and loneliness, conditions which could quickly lead to trouble for the unwary. The London Pass noted the name of the pass holder, his rank and details of his organisation and the time he would be allowed to remain off base. On the reverse side of the London pass, the following instructions were provided:

IMPORTANT INSTRUCTIONS FOR YOUR WELFARE

1. *Make arrangement for your accommodation immediately and know how to get back after the blackout. Check your extra gear and money before going out to see the Town.*

2. *Remember buses stop running at 10 p.m. and the Underground at 11 p.m.*

3. *If you have lost your return railway ticket, go to the R.T.O. at the Station. He can issue a Warrant to you.*

4. *WARNING! Do not buy your liquor from strangers and cheap private clubs.*

5. *Watch your pass and papers and DO NOT flash a roll of money.*

6. *Use the Red Cross Service Clubs Information Services. They are available.*

7. *If you are lost or need help, go to The Rainbow Club, Shaftesbury Avenue, off Piccadilly Circus – telephone Gerard 5616.*

8. *London Prophylactic Stations are at 101 Piccadilly, W.1 (Washington Club); 29 Sloane Street, S.W.1 (Hans Crescent Club); 63 St James's Street 7th Gen. Disp., 9 North Audley Street; and 9 Prince of Wales Terrace, W.8. (Milestone Club). Further directions can be obtained from porters or doormen at the American Red Cross Clubs.*

9. *Do not hesitate to ask any M.P. or London Bobby for directions. They know all the answers.*

Because London was the obvious place for the GI to spend a pass, the American Red Cross provided a variety of clubs offering food, accommodation and a warm welcome to 'Americans far from home'. The most famous

PASS TO LONDON
NOT to be shown to unauthorized persons   Pass No. **C** 17944

James A. Johnson
Name

T/Sgt.   20734697
Grade   *Serial No.*

Hq's 95th Bomb Gp   634
Organization   *APO No.*

                                    ┌ Pay
                    Pay status ┤ Class F
                                    └ Class B

Signature of Bearer   OVER

Bearer is authorized to be absent from his duties and station

from 1300   Sept 13 to 1300 Sept15
      Hour   *Date*   *Hour*   *Date*
inc., for the purpose of visiting London. It is understood
that this organization's allotment of beds at the A.R.C.

Moystn   Club
will not be reserved after 10 p.m. The bearer is aware
of the provisions of Cir. 69, ETOUSA, 30-10-42.

Signature of C.O.

                                    Rank

                                    OVER

PASS TO LONDON. *(Jim Johnson)*

club of all was the one for Enlisted Men known as 'Rainbow Corner', in Piccadilly. This was opened in November 1942 and at its peak was used by 30,000 men daily. A written history of the American Red Cross defined Rainbow Corner as a clearinghouse for all Red Cross activities in Britain:

> *It offered the best that the Red Cross could provide in the fields of recreation and entertainment. It did not have a dormitory, but made sleeping arrangements for the man through other clubs. As an indication of the size of the operation, on a single day in January 1944 over sixty thousand meals and half a million snacks were served. It was estimated that thirty thousand questions were asked daily at the information desk.*

There was much controversy at the time within the ARC as to whether there would be a charge for their services. Apparently, the ARC had campaigned for funds in the winter of 1941–42 on the grounds that the servicemen would not be required to pay. However, the *History of the American Red Cross* noted that

> *in March 1942, the Secretary of War sent the ARC a letter requesting the organisation to make a nominal charge for their services. The Central Committee of the Red Cross reluctantly agreed, but maintained that the clubs must operate at a loss and indeed a loss of $20,500 was shown at the end of 1943.*

Leroy Kuest resented the charge for accommodation at the American Red Cross because he could get a bed in a hotel for one pound and the ARC was charging one shilling (a twentieth of a pound) for a room with nineteen other beds. He felt that they were thus making the same profits as a commercial hotel and felt morally obliged not to patronise them.

The ARC did provide a superior service bearing in mind their specialist clientele. They operated information desks and hospitality desks for those who wanted to meet British families. Clothes could be laundered and pressed, shoes shined, and hair cut. All the clubs sold *Stars and Stripes* and *Yank* magazine. Furthermore, an extensive recreational programme was built up offering many kinds of sports, concerts, language lessons and excursions.

Some GIs still preferred private hotels and they were free to make that choice. Some liked the privacy, the softer beds and the better service, but above all they liked to get away from other GIs and anything to do with the Army Air Force. It seems that few were deterred by the price alone. Bert Stiles and his pilot Sam Newton opted for a good London hotel where, they 'lay on the green silk bedspreads ... and drank three double scotches'.

Harry Higel was not so fortunate. He became a regular guest at the Howard Hotel in London, but one day arrived to find that it was fully booked. He was offered and accepted a bathtub lined with bedsprings and when he checked out he joked with the staff that 'he had slept many times in a room with no bath, but never in a bath with no room!'

Freedom and privacy were important and some groups even went so far as to rent a flat in London for the use of their men when on leave, complete with a local woman to keep the place clean. It was also possible to achieve complete freedom by renting a flat for the duration of the leave and Charles Rankin, a Military Policeman, recalled that he rented a small apartment near Buckingham Palace – a basement flat – when on a week's leave. He enjoyed his time in London while staying there.

Apart from the ARC, which usually offered overnight accommodation, London boasted a range of clubs to suit all tastes. Most of them provided the much sought after bar and females. The Brevet catered for officers of all Allied nations, and there were Anglo-American clubs to promote integration on a social level.

Getting around London presented no problem to the Yanks. There was an adequate bus service and the underground operated as usual. Added to this there was a taxi service which was well utilised, if not commandeered by the GIs. Taxis were relatively cheap for the Americans, who jumped into them very frequently, often for quite lengthy journeys. This irritated the British who could not get a taxi when they needed one and led to the famous cartoon by Giles of the London *Daily Mail*. He portrayed a B17 crew having been shot down and standing on the kerbstone of a Berlin street confidently yelling 'Taxi!'

The 1943 book *Skyways to Berlin* noted that the taxi drivers in London were 'shabby, sullen, but efficient' and that a sixpenny tip was the accepted rate. Earlier on there had been a feud between the taxi drivers and the Yanks because 'the Yank is a generous tipper, but he objects to being re-minded, or having the recipient fix the amount'. Apparently, some cabbies passed Yanks by on rainy nights to get the message home and before too long, the Americans 'made their surrender generously'.

Although there were restaurants operating in the war, the limited ra-tions drastically reduced the available menu. They were always expensive. Steaks were not available (one moderate sized steak would have amounted to a week's meat ration for a family of four). The meat that was available was often a poor cut disguised in some way. John Appleby noted that he had a 'discouraging meal' at a restaurant in the City of Durham consisting of a slice of cold spam and a boiled potato. He found another restaurant where 'the only dish on the menu was sliced spam with boiled potatoes and greens'. Finding no satisfaction in the north of England, he returned to his base at Bury St Edmunds and found that lunch consisted of 'a slice of cold spam, a boiled potato and boiled greens'.

Towards the end of the War one of the big drawbacks of a night out in London was the V1 and V2 problem. These terror weapons, launched from the continental coastline, caused much havoc and destruction as well as loss of life. The V1 ('doodlebug') buzzed noisily overhead and it was only when the buzzing stopped, indicating that the engine had cut out, that the missile fell to earth and exploded. The V2 rocket was far more insidious in that it travelled faster than sound so that there was no warning of its ap-proach and it carried a much more powerful warhead.

For most Americans these weapons were a new and unwanted experi-ence and Earl Rudolph, an officer on leave in London, recalled one such occasion:

> I went to the Regent Palace Hotel where the only available room was on the top floor. After retiring, I heard the sirens followed by the noise of the buzz bombs (V1s). One hit short, the next one long. I jumped out of bed, put on pants and shoes at which time one hit awful close. The windows were blown out and the plaster came down. I ran downstairs to the subway where I spent the night. The next morning I returned to my base where the boss asked why I was home so soon. I replied: 'I've been and I'm back. I don't want to stay there'.

The GIs were amused at the stoical British temperament that was often revealed during these attacks. Dan O'Keefe remembered a bombing attack when he was eating in a restaurant and an elderly couple refused to leave their meal, becoming indignant at the situation. Afraid to look cowardly, Dan sat with them, but really wanted to run for cover. On another occasion, near panic ensued when a taxi containing three Yanks found itself in an area under attack. One of the passengers yelled for the taxi to stop, another for it to turn left and another for it to turn right. The driver just shook his head and drove on.

Unfortunately, it seems bombs were not the only hazard to be found in London. An officer stayed at a 'posh' London hotel after a run of missions, simply requiring a hot bath and some sleep in a soft bed. He 'caught a dose of scabies' and recalled: 'That was the last time I behaved like a Sunday School boy in London!'

Theatres and stage musicals were exceedingly popular attractions, as were the cinemas, although most of the films had been seen before in the USA. These occasions were sometimes interrupted by air raids, but generally life went on much as it always had. Dances were already a well-established leisure activity, but in London during the war they were an essential ingredient for the upkeep of morale. Robert Arbib noted that sometimes you were not sure whether you were dancing to the music or to the sound of anti-aircraft fire. The Opera House at Covent Garden had been converted into a temporary dancehall and was frequented by service personnel. Although these evenings were more impersonal than those at the local dancehalls around East Anglia, the girls were generally more sophisticated. Some were wild affairs and it was at Covent Garden where Dan O'Keefe remembered he 'used to dance on the tables'. They had a bar, but usually ran out of alcohol well before the end of the evening.

On a more sombre note, Dick Caroboneau went to Covent Garden dancehall to try to forget the loss of his good friend in combat. He was quietly drinking alone in a corner when he heard a soft voice behind him ask if he needed a friend. A young lady had noticed his sadness and was offering support. He said 'I almost cried,' but took her up on her offer and they finished up touring around the sites of London.

The girls of London were not generally pursued as possible steady girlfriends, but as one night stands. Although most were completely respectable, London was an easy place to find prostitutes. Almost certainly some men arrived in London with this in mind, but others were merely opportunists taking advantage of a unique situation. Two B24 gunners picked up two such women one evening and took them to a hotel for the night. In the morning at breakfast the girls were so foul-mouthed that the

PICCADILLY CIRCUS, 1944. *(Frank Halm)*

men were embarrassed. Having paid for the breakfast and the hotel bill, they left.

The darkened streets of Piccadilly, London, were home to many prostitutes. The blackout provided further hazards for the unwary visitor to the British capital. One veteran recalled the night when he and a friend got chatting to two girls in the dark and agreed to take them to dinner. He was with a friend in the blackout and someone put an arm round him and held on as a very feminine voice whispered in his ear: 'Want to have some fun Yank?' They agreed to get to know each other first over some food. At this stage he only knew that the person he was holding onto was a female by the smell of her perfume as it was so dark. In the light of the restaurant the two men were more than a little disappointed with their dates! He remembered their feelings at the time:

> *I led to a table and held the chair for my companion to be seated. Johnny did the same, then I noticed the look on his face as he looked at the girl seated opposite him, which happened to be my newly found 'girlfriend.' I looked at this 'friend' and did a double take. Now most of the English girls were just like the Americans; some pretty, some not, but these two . . . well, I just hoped that none of the fellows from our base happened to be in this place.*

The two men decided they were not hungry after all, and announced that they needed to 'use the bathroom' where they made their escape through a back door.

86

Bob Banta recalled that the 'Commandos'

abounded in great numbers in and around Piccadilly . . . you didn't have to look. They found you. Oh, how bold they were. On one of our trips to London, we had just arrived and stopped at a corner to let the traffic go by. Suddenly, the most handsomest and dignified member of our group went straight up in the air yelling 'Cut it out! Get out of here!' A typical Commando moved away with an amused look on her face. It seems that she had introduced herself by grabbing him rather roughly in the crotch and saying 'How about it Yank'.

James Bunch remembered that the London prostitutes carried small torches and beamed the light onto their ankles which became the standard form of recognition. It is said that the 'Commandos' would scale their charges according to rank after feeling for the insignia on the sleeve of their customers in the dark. The charges ranged from ten shillings to several pounds.

Jim McMahon, a very young gunner, recalled the time he went to London and watched the prostitutes emerge after dark:

One of my crew members gave me his wallet to hold after he had extracted £2 and I waited while he left with a girl. I was teased for this later, but I was satisfied to merely play the role of the banker – besides it was a very short wait.

Because of the sheer numbers of Americans in London and the fact that they generally had more money, they were often singled out and accosted by prostitutes in preference to men from other forces. Some of these girls would actually grab hold of an American to impress their solicitations. Although such advances were undoubtedly welcome at times, deflecting unwanted advances soon became good sport and one popular retort was 'Five pounds! I want to rent it, not buy it.' One group of Americans took their base chaplain for a tour around Piccadilly to assist his 'education'. A man of the cloth, with five children at home, the poor man provided much amusement from his discomfort.

Bert Stiles noted that the London prostitute

may be a hard-eyed bitch in the dawn, and she may put you away without pay for months (venereal disease), but when the mist is in your brain, and the war is yesterday and overhead and probably tomorrow, she is the princess of darkness.

One 'Commando' was actually leased by a GI for a whole week to enhance his leave while he was in London. She stayed with him exclusively for the whole time. In addition to her meals and hotel room, which of course they shared, he gave her a very generous £25. The fact that Americans were on average better off than servicemen from other countries often made them careless in their financial transactions. In November 1943, the *Stars and Stripes* carried an article which read:

> *Free-spending American soldiers who hand over half-a-crown for a shoe-shine, five to ten shillings for drink sold for half the price, were taken to task in a good humoured way by the London Daily Mail yesterday.*[Some tradesmen and taxi cabs were] *turning up their noses at old customers* [to give preference to Americans on leave in London] *with a pocketful of money and nothing in particular to spend it on.*

A London barber was now said to ride first class, smoke cigars and go to the theatre. He said:

> *I'm in the money . . . Twenty quid a week is easy to make now. Why, they* [the Yanks] *pay ten bob* [ten shillings] *for a haircut or ten bob for a shave.*

The newspaper did make the point that it understood most American soldiers spent their money sensibly, but there were plenty who did not.

Because British money was difficult to understand, cash was often handed over freely and with little excuse. It soon became apparent to any dishonest British person that it was a simple matter to part the GI from his money. One such example of this was when Dick Carboneau and a friend visited London. An English man approached them and asked them whether they had tickets to Petticoat Lane. They replied that they had not and when they expressed some interest, he offered to sell them some. He relieved them of half a crown each in return for 'tickets'. When the men arrived at Petticoat Lane and found it was no more than a famous street market, they realised they had been duped.

Due to the anonymity afforded by the size and darkness of wartime London, the criminal elements of society were well protected. Pickpockets and dishonest dealers were more common in London than in the provinces, and cigarette lighters were commonly stolen. Virtually unavailable to the British public and impossible to buy, they were a much prized possession at a time when most people smoked and they were consequently attractive to thieves Many Americans brought lighters with them from America, but soon learned not to leave them lying around on a bar or table. The PX occasionally sold lighters and fuel, but sometimes these were not available even there.

Fortunately for every rogue there were many Londoners who appreciated our American allies. On one occasion, a gunner was walking down a London street and was accosted by a British working man who thrust his own cigarette lighter upon the uncomfortable Yank in gratitude for American help in the war effort. The GI, realising the value of the gift, declined the offer with thanks. However, the English man did not give up and chased after the American with the lighter. Another man intervened and advised the Yank to accept it as it was intended as a genuine gift. The airman said he still could not bring himself to take the man's lighter. He just did not know what to do.

With little on the base to spend money on, it is not surprising that the average American arrived in London with a pocketful of notes and determined to have a good time. Some men were well organised enough to have cheque accounts in London banks. However, wartime rationing meant that there were limitations on the purchase of many items, even in London.

Another way to use money was to have the standard uniform personalised by a London tailor. The most common request was to have the blouse shortened to waist level and converted into what was called the 'Eisenhower Jacket'. The London tailors did good business with the Americans altering uniforms to personal specifications and even making completely new ones out of various fabrics.

The Hans Crescent Red Cross Club offered guided tours around London. The tour which left at 10 am took them to places of interest including Buckingham Palace, Downing Street, Westminster Abbey and St Paul's Cathedral. The leaflet informed

LONDON TOUR LEAFLET. *(Leroy Kuest)*

prospective customers that the tour would end up with a journey 'by under-ground from Westminster to Blackfriars, for the bombed areas of the City of London'.

A large proportion of American servicemen were distressed and per-turbed by the scale of destruction they found in London, but were struck by the determination of the British to continue to live as normally as pos-sible. Harry Higel witnessed a good example of this:

> *A sergeant and I went to London to pick up some new projection equipment and going out to the warehouse we travelled on an arterial street. Up ahead a V2 had exploded in a side street and the concussion came down that street full blast into a pub on the arterial street. It had knocked out all the windows, mirrors in the back bar, smashed tables and chairs, glassware and what have you. The Bobbies let us through and when we came back about an hour later, we were amazed to find the pub had been cleaned up and was back in business.*

One London pub provided much amusement for its American customers by the notice on the door which read: 'We remain open during air raids, but in the case of a direct hit, we will close immediately.'

Another feature of wartime London life which disturbed the American visitor was the number of civilians sheltering overnight in the underground stations. The Yanks remembered small children lying asleep on the plat-forms with trains screaming in and out. News broadcasts back home had not prepared the Americans for this and these scenes left them feeling powerless and frustrated, although Arbib noted that there were no signs of any 'nervous derangement' among the population of London. Londoners slept in the underground stations night after night, month in, month out and many found that in the morning they had no homes to return to.

Although the larger provincial towns had much to offer the GIs, London always offered more. Its tempo was faster, the people more cosmopolitan and the city itself positively throbbed with excitement. Even if men re-turned to base financially and physically depleted, this was seen to be a small price to pay for the wealth of experiences gained.

6

Stress and Fear

Fear was part of the furniture in every hut, in every pub, in every parlour, bedroom and bath in England.

ELMER BENDINER

Official sources show that only a small percentage of flying men were ever certified as psychological casualties although without doubt most airmen suffered a great deal of anxiety in relation to combat. It appears that whilst fear was not a subject widely or openly discussed between the men of the Army Air Force, its characteristic features were nevertheless apparent in many aspects of their attitudes and behaviour.

A certain amount of short-term stress in combat was not only desirable but also necessary, as it releases the hormone adrenaline which increases the pulse rate and helps in other ways to prepare the body for the dangers ahead. Crippling or excessive fear was rarely problematic during the heat of battle, but when it flared up away from the combat zone it could become damaging. Constant stress could have a negative effect on the body and depress the ability to think clearly.

Adverse reaction to stress was a serious concern and early in the war the Army commissioned three senior Medical Officers to look into this problem. Their report *Psychiatric Experiences of the Eighth Air Force – First Year of Combat* was published in 1944. Although fear was a burden which lay heavier upon some men than others, the Report does make the essential point that *the large majority of airmen tolerated these stresses in a normal manner, reacting with fear and tension in proportion to the degrees of stress involved, but without being psychiatric casualties. All airmen engaged in combat experienced fear.*

Many combat men found ways of relieving anxiety with psychological 'props' such as talismans and other superstitious practices, or by way of more physical releases such as alcohol and sex. Religion too played an important role for some.

If only for reasons of morale it is doubtful whether fear and other more negative aspects of aerial warfare were discussed in depth at training level. According to the 1944 report, 'new men did not accept fear as a possibility'. New fliers were nearly always eager to get into combat and were often frustrated if they hung about on the base for long prior to their first mission. Doubtless some nurtured a rather romantic notion of combat. New crews could usually be spotted by experienced GIs due to their misplaced eagerness and exuberance. It was not unusual for new blood to arrive convinced of their invulnerability, something which was important for their psychological well being at the time. They often disregarded any possibility of fear or danger. Bob Banta remembered his feelings at that time:

At first we were innocent and naive and thought that our crew was invincible. The first sight of a falling aeroplane was a rude awakening – not glamorous. You asked How the Hell did I get here?

This 'honeymoon' period did not usually last long, however, for any romantic notions of aerial combat were often dispelled on the first mission, particularly if it was a bad one. No type of training could prepare new men for the grim reality of this experience.

Fear was certainly played down in a 1944 article in the magazine *Air Force*. It stated that the 'American airman does not crack easily, even under the worst conditions', and even more ludicrously, that in a year and half of furious fighting, there had been just one case of a flier developing a true psychosis. The article blatantly plays on the macho and patriotic image that the Americans had of themselves. It tells of a 'dynamic stability in the average combat flier' and of the 'important factor of his individual pride'.

The typical airman is a handpicked specimen whose life has been characterised by more vigor, persistence and self-respect than the average person's. Such an individual is not likely to admit to himself that he can fall down on a job – or to enjoy living with himself if he does . . . There is plenty of danger left in the skies over Europe today. The Air War is still tough. But the men America is sending to do the job are equal to it.

Feelings of anxiety could affect the individual at any time during his tour of duty, but most agreed that the feelings of greatest tension were experienced in the run up to a mission, and most acutely during the preceding night. Once battle commenced there was little time to think about anything other than the job at hand and surviving. Bert Stiles noted that the time between stations (arrival at the aircraft) and take-off was difficult, as it allowed the opportunity to dwell on the coming mission.

Stations at four, take off at five, means there is usually a good part of any hour at the plane with nothing to do. The gunners have to put in their guns, and oxygen has to be checked, and the bombs loaded, but the ground crews do all the work, or already have it done. There is plenty of time to think in that hour.

The first couple of missions I used to lie there and twist myself around thinking about the flack and the 109 and 190s . . . and JU 88s and rocket guns and flak and ME 410s.

This is a quick way to go nuts.

After that I worked out a pretty good system. I'd find a nice quiet place outside on the grass under a wing, or out behind the tail and lie down with a flak suit for a pillow.

The night before I'd copy down the words of some song I wanted to know the words to and lie out there in the mornings and whistle it a couple of times and go through the words . . . It didn't matter much what, just so it was slow and sort of low down, so I'd be thinking about some dame instead of the B-one-seven.

The first few missions gave men their first taste of adventure and excitement. The *Psychiatric Experiences* report told of an 'overswing' which airmen experienced after four or five missions. By this time they often deplored their former 'cocky' attitude and became conscious of a new state of anxiety and they often felt quite hopeless about their chances of survival. However, the report goes on to say that by the tenth raid the individual 'had experienced fear and by now knew that he could deal with it . . . He developed an "esprit de corps" in regard to his squadron.' At this point the report seems to completely lose touch with reality claiming that fear in combat became less

93

pronounced, and consequently less of a problem, as more missions were completed. Veterans remembered feeling quite the opposite in that as more missions were successfully completed, often with narrow escapes, their luck could not hold out much longer. Dick Carboneau remembered:

The longer I survived, the greater seemed the odds against my survival. Meanwhile, the character of my fear was changing. While in the beginning it was mainly of my precious body being hit, it was now evolving into a fear of the aeroplane being shot down. Perhaps I was more afraid of being captured than killed or wounded. We didn't really know at the time what the Germans were doing to downed airmen they captured. I would have done just about anything to be able to quit and go home. Anything but ground myself, that is.

I once thought about disconnecting my oxygen mask at altitude just to escape the acute anguish – suicide – totally painless. However, I realised that I really cared about living and that was part of the fear. I just lived scared and tried not to show it. Nobody wanted to be 'chicken' but I'm willing to bet almost everyone felt at time that he was. It's probably a good thing we were contained in an aeroplane where we couldn't turn and run, because I might have.

Al Jones remembered that morale was pretty low whilst he was in England and that 'very few of us really ever felt that we COULD complete a tour – to us, a goal totally unreachable'.

Jim Sheller wrote home to his wife in 1944:

I'll tell you why I seem 'detached' in my letters. I'm scared, nervous and facing an ordeal that few humans ever do. I'm getting so close to the end that I hate to take a little chance.

Jim McMahon recalled that towards the end, he was becoming 'very skittish and developed a feeling of doom – being a fatalist and not worrying until my number was up, was not working anymore'.

Dan O'Keefe admitted that

With each mission I kept expecting the worst. As friends were either shot down or finished their tour of duty and went home, I made few new ones. I was turning inward more and more. I wasn't writing home much either. I couldn't express what I was experiencing; a thing so large that anything else was trivial.

94

My last mission was almost anticlimactic, although I managed to get more than my share of the flight surgeon's booze and got stiff as a plank.

The only complete relief from fear was to complete the prescribed amount of missions; 25 at the beginning of the war, but later increased to 30, then 35. Although many fliers were only in England for a matter of months, the time could seem interminable. That final mission and the feeling of elation which followed remained firmly etched in the minds of most veterans. On landing at the base, some literally fell out of the aeroplane in an effort to become re-established with the ground. Others shrieked and shouted and kissed the ground. One gunner actu-

DAN O'KEEFE, GUNNER, 93RD BOMB GROUP, BASSINGBOURN. *(Dan O'Keefe)*

ally put his feet out of the waist door and dragged them along the ground before the aeroplane had come to a halt. Bert Stiles wrote that he wanted to take his shoes off to feel the ground with his feet. One man was viewed by colleagues as a deadly serious, unsmiling man – until he flew his final mission whereupon he was 'born again, smiling, cheerful and happy'.

The Psychiatric Experiences report also claimed that 'there was no true malingering'. However, many veterans recalled that some missions were aborted with very little excuse. This was also experienced by RAF crews.

Sometimes men feigned sickness once they knew the mission target for that day, although this was usually met with little sympathy from

SGT E MISCHLER LOOKING VERY HAPPY HAVING COMPLETED HIS 25TH AND FINAL MISSION. 94TH BOMB GROUP. *(Courtesy of Norma Slater)*

colleagues. Conversely, certain men carried on as usual whilst suffering the most extraordinary physical symptoms of stress, as they were unable to admit these problems, even to themselves. Swellings of the face and limbs, hair loss and behavioural changes were sometimes experienced and nightmares and insomnia were suffered by many. Neurosis occasionally manifested itself in otherwise stable men, causing depression and a feeling of rejection by society. One airman was seen to be constantly and unnecessarily repairing his uniform, and another obsessively read his Bible all the time. Their crew members knew something was wrong with these men, but chose not to interfere.

There were no court martial proceedings for refusing to fly, and although a man could ground himself at any time it was unusual for this to happen. It meant demotion and a ground job for the duration of the war, and after having invested so much mental and physical energy in combat it was not an easy decision to make. Bob Banta wrestled with this problem for some time and it was noticed and remembered by a fellow crewman:

After a particularly rough mission, this man was seen to keep laying on his bed to contemplate something and then go to the door. After pausing for a moment at the door, he would return to the bed to contemplate further and then repeat the whole process several times. Eventually he threw himself on

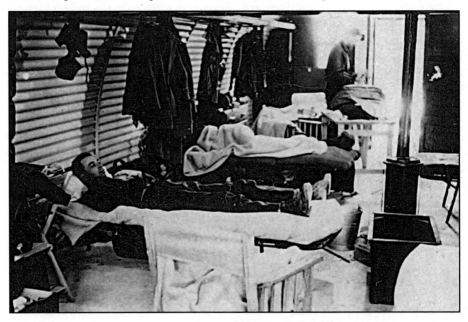

GI RESTING INSIDE NISSEN HUT. DETAILS UNKNOWN. *(USAF)*

his bed and exclaimed out loud 'Oh, to Hell with it. If I get killed, I get killed.'

Dick Carboneau recollected that when he did admit to himself that he was afraid, the last people he could tell were his crewmates in case they lost confidence in him and his work. Other veterans recollected that one's crewmates were the only people who understood, as you had to be going through it yourself to know how it felt.

Excessive fear and anxiety often produced feelings of isolation and low mood which were difficult, or even impossible, to express to others. In the absence of wives, mothers and girlfriends men sometimes turned to British civilians for support and they were usually more than willing to respond. The fliers often appreciated someone on the ground that cared about their personal welfare, and who would worry about them during missions and be relieved at their safe return. This did not have to be a male–female relationship, although it often was.

Even the most rational of men felt that they could not afford to ignore the value of any aid to morale in these circumstances. The most widely held superstition of them all was 'never volunteer'. There were many incidents that helped to reinforce these attitudes. For example Dick Carboneau remembered:

In our hut there was a big tough Texan named Dillon who liked to drink and fight, but was basically a pretty decent guy. One time he went to town and came back very late and so drunk that he couldn't be roused to fly a mission. So a friend who wasn't posted to fly volunteered in Dillon's place. That crew was shot down that day.

Dillon didn't seem to react much to that, at least not outwardly. He went on and finished his tour, and then volunteered to fly one more mission, from which he did not return.

In another incident, Dick remembered that a GI lost all his money in a card game. In frustration, he threw down his empty wallet on the table and said: 'I won't need this anymore' (because he had no money left to put into it). The next day he was shot down and killed. The men who knew him found this very disturbing and kept remembering the flier's words 'I won't need this anymore' as if it had been an omen.

Personal rituals were taken seriously, such as the method and order of dressing. One combat man remembered wearing the same set of underpants for the whole tour of duty (around 30 missions) – never washing them. It was usual to want to wear the same clothes, as if the fact that they had survived so far wearing a particular T-shirt or scarf for example, somehow ensured their future safety.

A popular though rather macabre idea which was officially prohibited was the money jar. Two men, each from different crews, would regularly put a set amount of cash into a jar, say two shillings a week. If they both survived, they would celebrate with these funds, but if one was shot down, the money would be claimed by the survivor who would take it to the bar and toast his lost friend. Bob Banta and a friend from another crew had a money jar between them. However, Bob was very upset when his friend was killed in action, but even more so when he went to locate the money to toast his friend and discovered that it had been stolen.

The United States Government provided good life insurance for combat men, and Dan O'Keefe recalled feeling that if he did get killed, it was a relief for him to know that his family would receive his death payment.

Precious photographs, letters and personal objects such as Bibles, crosses and items of women's underwear were taken into combat for good luck. Jim Lorenz, a Liberator pilot, regularly ate half a chocolate bar before leaving with the idea that he would eat the remainder at the end of that day. It was also common practice to leave precious objects with friends, girlfriends, or other British civilians on the understanding that you would 'have to come back to collect it'. Sadly, many of these items were never reclaimed.

It was considered bad luck for a man to have his photograph taken just before a mission and that his belongings should never be left too tidy as it might tempt fate by making it easy for the supply people to pack them up.

The novelist John Steinbeck was a war correspondent at the time and noted the importance of talismans when working with bomber crews in England. He wrote about this for an American newspaper and later republished the article in his book *Once there was a War*:

> *It is a bad night in the barracks, such a night as does not happen very often. It is impossible to know how it starts. Nerves are a little thin and no one is sleepy. The tail gunner of the other outfit in the room gets down from his upper bunk and begins rooting about on the floor.*
>
> *'What's the matter?' the man on the lower bunk asks.*
>
> *'I lost my medallion', the tail gunner says.*
>
> *No one asks what it was, a St. Christopher, or a good luck piece. The fact*

of the matter is that it is his medallion and he has lost it. Everyone gets up and looks. They move double-decker bunks out from the wall. They empty all the shoes. They look behind the steel lockers. They insist that the gunner go through all his pockets. It isn't a good thing for a man to lose his medallion. Perhaps there has been an uneasiness before. This sets it. The uneasiness creeps all through the room. It takes the channel of being funny. They tell jokes; they rag one another. They ask shoe sizes of one another to outrage their uneasiness. 'What size shoe you wear Brown? I get them if you conk out.' This thing runs bitterly through the room.

And then the jokes stop.

For the married man in combat there seems to have been a rather greater risk of psychiatric breakdown. Due to the rapid enlistment programme following the United States' entry into the war, it was common for many young couples to wed in haste. A man had little time in which to establish a relationship with his new wife, and parting was nearly always traumatic. A further complication was that many of these young men left their wives pregnant, or with young children, separation from whom added to their stress.

Combat men received enhanced salaries from the United States Government and for whatever reasons young husbands went into combat, the extra flying pay must have been particularly welcome for the newlyweds, especially after the years of economic depression. The married man would be less likely to ground himself than his single counterpart, simply because this would have protracted his stay in England.

Religion helped many combat men to cope with their fears and anxieties. Most bases were served by two chaplains, one Protestant and one Catholic. A chaplain was always available before a mission went out, the time when spiritual comfort and reassurance was most appreciated. Al Jones remembered that early morning communion was a 'comforting blanket of security'. Chaplains would often stand at the beginning or the end of the runway blessing each aeroplane as it took off. One even carried his own talisman, a red, white and blue horseshoe which he clasped as he waved the men off. Another performed amusing antics beside the runway in order to raise a smile from the crews before take-off.

Bob Banta remembered receiving solace from a religious experience which gave him the strength to carry on regardless of the final outcome. In a state of high anxiety over his next mission, he walked to the local village in Suffolk and sat for a while on a bench near to the church praying silently.

The month was June and he remembered the hedgerows strewn with poppies. He said a sense of serenity overcame him and he returned to base with a feeling of well-being and resignation over what might happen.

Dan O'Keefe recalled that

We had one man who, before take-off, would pace up and down in front of the aeroplane in silent prayer. But it was not the answer for me and perhaps not for him either; he was shot down.

Although religion was sometimes invoked as an antidote to fear, it also helped many airmen face up to their possible mortality. Not surprisingly, combat men thought about death a great deal as a result of losing friends and colleagues and being confronted with suddenly vacant bunks.

Anxiety often resulted in a pessimistic or even nihilistic attitude about the future. Death was seen as almost certain by some men. Even more insidious than the fear of death itself was the inability to predict precisely which form it would take. Bravery came in many forms, from a mortally wounded man quietly accepting his fate to the more dramatic manhandling of a burning aircraft. No one knew what opportunities for bravery would be presented to them, nor how well or badly they would cope. Few wanted to be tested. Undoubtedly, horrific events were mulled over and the inevitable question would arise: 'What if that had been me?'

Bert Stiles, who thought about this a good deal, personified death as a 'lady' in his book:

Sometimes she's a screaming horrible bitch . . . And sometimes she's a quiet one, with soft hands that rest gently on top of yours on the throttle.

Fear was intricately interwoven with morale and when men became crippled by tensions and anxiety, their morale plummeted. The loss of a close friend, or a 'Dear John' letter from home, could heighten an individual's anxiety and heavy losses within a squadron, or group, sapped morale.

Some men sought less spiritual palliatives in the form of drink and sex. Some airmen did not drink, but those that did often deliberately consumed too much, believing perhaps (as the *Psychiatric Experiences* report says) that 'overindulgence was a cathartic sort of release of feelings, which they felt to be useful'.

Alcohol was even used officially by the Army Air Force to relax combat men on return from a mission, prior to debriefing. Dick Carboneau, who was a very young gunner at the time, remembered:

When we returned from a mission they had a bar set up in the debriefing room and every man received coffee, tea, or a measured shot of Scotch before talking to the intelligence officers. I always knew who did not drink and had them get me their ration of Scotch. Sometimes, I'd have as many as seven or eight shots. Then afterwards I'd return to my empty barracks and sleep until late at night. I'd then go to the Sergeants' club and drink ale until I was thoroughly soused and hope I wasn't going out on a mission the next day.

Men who were completely shattered with exhaustion at the end of a combat day still somehow found the energy to go to a club on base, or the local pub. Harry Slater remembered that some officers would regularly pass out from drink at the base club and the 'medics would simply take them to their bunk'. For the drinking man, alcohol was an easy short-term remedy for the pressures of combat. Dan O'Keefe recalled:

I went to the Sergeant's pub and got drunk every night. I might meet someone that I thought I knew. It really didn't matter if I knew them or not by then because we just got drunk together and talked about what missions we'd been on.

Many combat men admitted that they went into combat still feeling the effects of the night's drinking. A celebrated, and apparently very effective, remedy for a hangover, was to put the individual oxygen supply on 'rich'.

Harry Slater said that he would not have taken any crew member into combat if he was obviously drunk or groggy, but a Liberator pilot remembered well how he himself suffered after a night out whilst on a late flying schedule. He had only just returned to base and fallen asleep in his bed when he was woken up for what would be his longest mission ever: 'I suffered through nine hours and went to bed as soon as we got back'. Bob Banta recalled the evening when three crewmates acquired a bottle of Scotch whilst on a 48-hour pass to London. They hitched a lift back to the base drinking all the while, and giving drinks to their lifts. Arriving at 1.30 a.m. Bob checked to see if they were lucky enough to have been placed on a late schedule for flying the next day: 'I was relieved to see that we were not listed – having to rely on that lot for my life, I was not looking forward to.'

One option for the prevention and cure of excessive tension was the Rest Homes for combat men run by the American Red Cross. Combat fatigue had been described in World War 1 and labelled 'shell shock'. However, the euphemism adopted by the Yanks was 'flack happy' and thus the Rest

Homes became known as the 'Flack Shacks' or 'Flack Houses'. Here, it was hoped, men would be able to enjoy some Rest and Recuperation (known as R & R). The *Psychiatric Experiences* report recognised the importance of this and recommended an ideal set up:

> *In the Rest Homes, the military atmosphere should be kept to a minimum. Civilian clothes should be furnished, and men should be allowed to get up in the morning whatever time pleases them and breakfast should be served accordingly. Equipment for sports and games should be available, but the men should not be pushed into these activities, if for example, they would rather sit and read or sleep . . . The food should be better both in quality and preparation than the men can get on their own stations, the beds should be good, and there should be adequate bathing facilities. They may appear to be small points but they are the aspects of a Rest Home that the men seem to appreciate the most.*

The value of Rest Homes was recognised early in the War. In the first years of combat, there were only two such establishments, one for officers and one for enlisted men. By the end of the War, however, Red Cross records show around 20 such facilities in existence.

The *Psychiatric Experiences* report recommended that men should be sent to Rest Homes at about midway point in their operational tour. However, it pointed out that there was a problem in getting the men to go in the first place. The Homes, as they stood, were not particularly attractive to many young combat men. Country mansions and houses were requisitioned by the British Government for the use of the Red Cross and consequently many were in remote rural areas. One exception was the Palace Hotel in Southport, near Blackpool, which was on the seafront of a fair sized northern seaside town. Certainly it was in the interest of the Military to make these places as attractive as they could so that the men returned to combat duty as refreshed as possible. Even so, there was always some resistance from the proposed guests.

Elmer Bendiner noted in *A Fall of Fortresses* how grudgingly his crew accepted the idea: 'we were shipped to Blackpool as if we were machine parts that had to be chipped and overhauled'.

A bomber pilot, Hubert McMillan, felt so strongly about it that he separated from his crew and went to London for the week.

A B17 pilot wrote in his diary of his experience at Southport Rest Home: 'Southport is nice in the day time, but Bob and I have seen every show in town and the pub is full of noisy GIs.' At the end of that week he wrote to his wife: 'Tomorrow we have to go back, which is a terrible thing except there'll be letters from you.' He also noted that 'the crew is finding this spot a bit dull and are going to London to finish their leave.' A pilot remembered being thoroughly bored, although his stay was early on in the war and perhaps before the Rest Homes became fully operational. His group also had to put up with the sound of artillery fire from a British anti-aircraft training base from early in the morning and then all day. Things picked up for

FRANK HALM WITH A FRIEND AT THE PALACE HOTEL, A REQUISITONED REST HOME IN SOUTHPORT. *(Frank Halm)*

him, however, when he was seduced by a waitress in one of the small local restaurants!

Some GIs saw R & R as literally a waste of time as they were anxious to get on with the job and complete their tour of duty. A fair proportion of the men that visited the facilities were appreciative and made full use of them. Some memories from those times include a Mustang pilot, Bert McDowell:

We went to Southport – lots of women and drink. It was nice to have linen, table service and sheets again, even for just a week.

Two B17 gunners also had a great time. One wrote:

We went to Leicestershire. A nice week's vacation at a lovely English mansion staffed by pretty young Red Cross Workers. It was about as unmilitary as they could make it; we wore casual civvies, had no duties, did pretty much as we pleased. The food was excellent, prepared by a rare individual – an army cook with the real soul of an artist.

And the other wrote:

I didn't want to go. Went to the country in the middle of England somewhere.

After I had been there two days, I didn't want to leave. A Butler would wake us up and say 'Good Morning Sir – it's a beautiful day outside.' We played tennis and ping-pong with the Red Cross girls. We danced with them and went on walks and bike rides. That week did me a lot of good. I didn't realise it, but I needed it. When I came back I was refreshed physically and mentally.

Sending fliers to the Rest Homes at the recommended time of halfway through their tour of duty this did not always work to the individual's advantage. Jim McMahon said that his trip to the Rest Home came too early on in his tour of duty:

It was a lovely week, but I didn't really need the vacation at the time nearly so much as I would later on when I couldn't have it.

Worse still was the fact that some fliers actually missed out completely on R & R. Some of these arrived early in the war before the R & R system had begun, but as the war progressed, it was possible that some groups could not spare the men from combat duty. As late as 1988, a veteran wondered if he could collect that trip after more than 40 years as he felt that the American Government still owed him one!

It appears that all too often men were driven to the limits of endurance by their combat experiences. Bert Stiles wrote that he broke down and cried before he was sent for R & R and a young gunner thought that the Flight Surgeon arranged his Rest when he was seen to spill the post-mission Scotch when he tried to drink it. For some it was just too late and Elmer Bendiner gave a vivid account of one such case in his book. The crew had arrived at their Rest Home town by aeroplane and he was on the tarmac waiting for the rest of his crew to alight:

They emerged from the waist of the aeroplane carrying something. They gathered in a circle around whatever it was. I elbowed into the group and saw at our feet our ball turret gunner, Leary, the youngest of the crew. His hands clutched empty air. His eyes rolled back beneath his lids exposing a fish-white vitreous. His shirt was pulled away from his trousers, and the belt pinched the skin of his belly purple. His neck and face were splotched.

Keep him warm . . . give him air, people shouted. Bohn and Mike were kneeling at Leary's side. Bohn was trying to take hold of Leary's tongue to keep his airway open. Someone asked for a coat. I took mine off and handed it to Bohn, who covered Leary. Then some RAF groundling tore up in an ambulance and loaded Leary aboard a stretcher . . . Leary was asserting, with purple epileptic emphasis, that he would fly and fight no more.

Most men found their own way of coping and just lived with the tension. A change of scene was often enough, as in a 48-hour leave, but certainly the Rest Homes proved successful for many. Whether they were universally appreciated or not, they did play an important role in the treatment and relief of anxiety and stress. At the very least they offered the combat man an extremely pleasant and comfortable week's vacation.

Whilst combat men were away at the Rest Homes and hopefully forgetting about the war, others were still flying and dying from the bases they had left behind. The men from each crew often shared a hut with several other crews, and whether returning from a Rest Home, leave, or a mission, it was a traumatic experience for them to learn that their friends were either Missing in Action, or had been killed. Jim McMahon recalled that on one occasion, 'the beds upon returning were rumpled just like they left them that morning to fly. We tried to ignore them.'

The *Psychiatric Experiences* report did not ignore the seriousness of the problem and went so far as to suggest that huts had partitions containing two to three beds only in the hope that this would make it easier for men to bed down early before a mission and help disguise battle losses.

There is no evidence that these recommendations were ever implemented. The RAF had a policy of 'full breakfast table' which meant that men from other tables sat on the seats of those who had been killed, thus making the losses less obvious. It took a while for the Americans to get organised in this respect. It was a common experience for combat men not to want to get too close to members from other crews. One combat man complained that no one had prepared him for the appalling losses. Hubert McMillan remembered that on these occasions, there was a burning desire to get away from the base:

> *It reached a point where we didn't want to know each other that well, at least from the other crews, because we only lost them anyway. There was a high turnover of combat men and with each crew moving into our hut, we became more distant. It became easier to leave the base to avoid close friendships. We were close to our own crewmates. We had to be.*

Often the first indication of a missing colleague was when the property officer came to the hut to collect his personal belongings. This was a sad and demoralising experience. The men who cleared out lockers and cupboards were often told not to send home pin-ups belonging to the missing man, which might have accumulated on the walls behind the bunks, for fear that these might embarrass his relatives. However, Bob Banta recalled that if word had got around first, it was unlikely that there would be anything incriminating there:

> When a man was Missing In Action, official procedure was for the Supply Officer's people to collect all GI and personal belongings, the latter to be boxed up and sent to his next of kin. Unofficially, his buddies usually went through his stuff first, particularly in the case of a married man, to remove letters, photos or such from any girlfriends he might have had along the way. Just an act of kindness to spare his family needless extra pain.

The loss of a particular friend was naturally a particularly difficult experience. Jim McMahon said he would never forget the day that his close friend and crew member was killed when his aeroplane exploded whilst flying with another crew:

> When Fred was killed, the enlisted men of our crew went down to the flight line and stayed long after dark waiting for him to return. It was a strange thing to do because we knew he was dead. We packed his things ourselves and would not let anyone else outside of our crew touch any of his belongings. I inherited his short boots which he had purchased in Natal, Brazil. He had told me to take them if anything ever happened to him. They were a size too small for me, but I wore them when I went to town a few times even though they hurt my feet.

Dick Carboneau had a similar experience in losing a former crew member who had flown with another crew. He had also been on a mission that day and heard about his friend's death at debriefing:

> At first it didn't quite sink in, but I kept thinking about Don, wondering how much of what I'd heard was fact, and why I seemed to feel nothing. I went down to the flight line, found Suther's [the pilot's] plane and looked inside. There on the floor of the radio room was a very large puddle of blood, the last of Don that I was ever to see. Then I turned away and cried. Two days later on a gray, chilly, rainy day, Don was buried at a military cemetery a few miles from the base. All of us who knew him were there. Row on row of flag-draped coffins lay beside freshly dug graves in that sodden, grassless burying ground. Rites were said simultaneously by Protestant, Catholic and Jewish Chaplains. A salute was fired, taps sounded, and we returned to our bases.

7

The Ground Echelon

We who were the paddlefeet were privileged to be near the fighting line and to do our jobs alongside the combat men. The results of our efforts showed up to us in successful missions and lives saved.

ALLAN HEALY

The ground crews generally experienced a longer, quieter war than their flying colleagues but their longer tours of duty were not without drama and even horror. Although combat-related deaths were usually felt most acutely by the flyers themselves such losses reverberated throughout the base and had an adverse psychological effect on everyone. Those confined to the ground often witnessed aircraft crashes during take-off or limping back to base with dead, dying or injured airmen on board.

In 1944, a Group Commander was concerned that the aviators were getting all the write-ups whilst the ground men were being quietly overlooked. He knew that without the work of the 'unseen army' no bomber would ever have taken off from the British Isles and, although he knew that their skills and dedication were certainly appreciated on the base, he was keen for this to be more widely recognised. To this end a booklet entitled *On Base* was published in the series 'Army Talks for the 8th Air Force'.

Ground personnel, popularly known as 'Paddlefeet,' 'Groundgrippers' and 'Gravel Crunchers', appeared as somewhat less glamorous than the aircrews – they wore no wings on their chests and worked long hours outside in all weathers. They were stationed in Britain for the duration of the war.

GROUND STAFF SWEATING OUT A MISSION: 94TH BOMB GROUP, ROUGHAM.
(USAF)

According to the 94th Bomb Group history, however, they were 'the life blood of the operation'. The book *Target Germany*, produced by the US Army Air Forces, also recognised that the 'paddlefeet' were undervalued.

In some ways the men on the ground had the short end of the stick, especially the enlisted men. There was no glory in the anonymous but necessary job of packing a parachute or driving a truck or guarding a Fortress in the rain-swept hours between midnight and dawn. Nobody handed out medals to the man who picked the sullen, slippery bombs out of the mud and washed them off, so that no blemish should keep them from falling true and hoisted them into the yawning bomb bays with apparatus that had been known to slip and let a thousand-pound bomb fall and crush the bomb loader's feet. Nobody complimented the weary-eyed assistants in the photo labs, working frantically to get the bomb-strike photos of the day's mission processed in a minimum of time. Nobody wrote glamorous newspaper stories about the cooks.

Chuck Galian, an aircraft mechanic, remembered that the work of the ground echelon was not without danger:

Bombs being loaded in the rain were liable to slip in wet hands and guns needed careful handling whilst loading and unloading. Accidental gunfire from parked aircraft was not uncommon.

A terrible incident occurred on the base at Alconbury, near Cambridge. Whilst bombs were being loaded, one exploded, setting up a chain reaction of further explosions. Nineteen men were killed, 18 'shocked beyond belief' and an armourer, who arrived soon after, was horrified to see a dog with human ribs it its mouth.

Some of the ground men received medals as the 8th Air Force Commander recognised the great job they were doing. Vernon Ellis, a mechanic, remembered that

> the 'Bronze Star' was created and several crew chiefs were awarded this. It was awarded when an aircraft flew 100 missions without ever having to abort (turn back early) due to a mechanical failure, or malfunction.

Allan Healy noted that

> Approximately three ground men worked for every aircrew man that crossed the enemy coast in a plane. We know that the ground personnel worked hard, but this work was not always obvious.

He gave an illuminating account of this work in the few hours prior to a mission:

GROUND MEN BOMB LOADING, HARDWICK. *(Jim McMahon)*

Some time before midnight the Division Field order would come across the teletype and from the communications center and operations head-quarters, would go a maze of orders. The dispatcher would call his telephone checklist and the section officers and enlisted men on for the night shift would bend to their work. Communications would be preparing the Radio Operator's flimsies, giving the colors of the day, call signals, and emergency procedures, and preparing the Radio Operator's briefing. Weather, who had been checking steadily and engaging in many conference telephone calls, would confer again and Cloudy Lindstrom would get his charts lined and the cross section of clouds-to-the-target ready for the briefing baloptican. Photo installed its one vertical camera for every three or four planes and assigned the gunner's hand-held K-20s for oblique shots. The motor pool had to be ready to pick up the crews in the pre-dawn dark, take them to breakfast, to briefing, and out to the planes on the perimeter strip. The mess hall must break out the real eggs for the flyboys' breakfast and satisfy the on-duty personnel, who would wander in during the night for something to fortify them. The MPs are ready to guard the briefing buildings. Radar loaded chaff and checked the G-boxes.

This does not take into account the changes of orders concerning the bomb load at various stages of loading, the cold, the wet, and the many difficulties encountered . . . This was a hard night's work . . . The Paddlefeet get little recognition, but theirs is a story of devotion to duty.

ORDNANCE WORKER, 94TH BOMB GROUP, ROUGHAM. *(Frank Halm)*

The ground-based men never had the experience of dropping the bombs on the target, shooting down an enemy fighter, or bringing a shot-up aircraft safely into land, but they did have the satisfaction of knowing that their efforts had helped to make these things possible. They were not a faceless group of men. Bonds between the two groups were strong as ground crew were often the last human beings a bomber crew saw before take off and the first they saw on return. The bomber crews were not forgotten while they were away on a mission either, because in most cases the ground crews would have been 'sweating out' the mission for the duration and would be relieved and thrilled at the sight of the returning bombers.

Contemporary news reports are partly to blame for the low profile of the ground echelon because they were constantly supplying the American people with stories of fearlessness and gallantry in combat for propaganda purposes. Those fliers returning to their hometown after their tour of combat duty were welcomed back as returning heroes. In most cases the war was still in progress and very much in the public mind – these men were perceived to have diced with death in the defence of liberty.

News reports on life in a bomber station in England were broadcast in the USA throughout the war, but these nearly always centred on the combat men. No one wrote about the cooks, the administrators, or intelligence personnel. Their history did not make good 'copy'.

Non-fliers were not a cohesive group of men in the same way as the aviators and had little in common with each other apart from the fact that they did not go into combat. Those who actually serviced the aeroplanes were closest to the action so it is not surprising that they generally enjoyed a closer relationship with the combat men. Some ground crews cherished the notion that the aeroplane was really theirs and they lent it to the aircrews each day. Sometimes the pilots were humorously 'reprimanded' by the mechanics for returning the aircraft full of holes!

Many mechanics built a 'line shack' near to the hard stand where their aeroplane was parked and where they worked on it. The shacks were made from very basic materials such as recycled packing crates and were used by the mechanics as somewhere to rest during the day, or even to sleep overnight. For some, it was easier than returning to the barracks.

It was unusual for aircrews to mix socially with the ground men. This was due mainly to the logistics of not being in the same place at the same time and, of course, army protocol. The sharing of experiences was a necessary ingredient for firm and enduring friendships. John McLane, in his unpublished book *Thirty One Missions from a Navigator's Viewpoint*, noted:

I noticed there was no effort from the ground crews to get close to us. Anyone could tell there was mutual admiration between us, but I suspect we flying men lived in our own dream world and that the ground crews had seen too many of their 'friends' not return.

Vernon Ellis remembered:

A B17 was made up of four officers and six enlisted men. Of course we rarely mixed socially with the officers, although there was rarely any snobbery involved on their part. They respected us and if they had any complaints they would normally take them to the officer in charge of maintenance who would discuss the incident with us. As for the enlisted flight crew members we were very close to the original crews with whom we trained in the States. We remained close after arriving in England, but each time one of them was lost in combat it was too painful so we didn't get close to the replacement crews. Besides after the air war speeded up and they came and went faster there was little opportunity to get acquainted. Sometimes on nice days when the crew was not flying and we were doing some major work (like an engine change) the flight engineer might ride out on his bicycle to watch, and sometimes even the pilot. More than one crew member (even officers) would come out

LINE SHACK, 44TH BOMB GROUP, SHIPDHAM. *(Al Jones)*

to sleep off a bad hangover in one of our line shacks where privacy was assured compared to the barracks. We were very careful not to disturb them. Anything we could do to ease the tension they were under was OK with us.

Tony North remembered that enlisted men were discouraged from socialising with officers. He lived near to the 467th Bombardment Group at Rackheath in Norfolk where he said the Green Man pub was for the use of officers and the Sole and Heel for enlisted men. Apparently, 'they would leave Rackheath if they wanted to drink together'.

One mechanic remembered that he actually felt guilty about the combat men and the fact that he had a safer job. He had been turned down for gunnery training due to colour blindness. Another recalled that:

We looked up to them, but they did not look down on us. All they wanted was the best equipment in the best condition we could keep it . . . We did not mix socially with combat men – we lived apart and ate apart. They had their friends and we had ours. We might meet them in a pub sometimes, but that was about all. You tended to buddy up with the fellows you worked with. We talked about different things. They talked about flying, ever cold and ever scared – about fighter plane attacks, about flack bursting all around – about the next plane getting it and going down. We had nothing to say that could match their stories.

The fact that the ground crews were held in high esteem by fliers is undisputed. Leroy Kuest noted in his diary at the time that some crews flying in from North Africa brought back watermelons and cantaloupes for their colleagues. On one base a parachute packer received a gift from the mother of a shot down gunner. The gunner had written to her from his POW camp asking her to find the packer and reward him because the parachute had saved his life.

The ground crews at one Norfolk base came by an unexpected reward as recalled by Jim Sheller when he was returning from Italy:

Our bomb bays were filled with cases of bootleg champagne and brandy from Foggia. We were briefed to England via the Bay of Biscay at low level. I insisted that we went straight home over the French Alps and at 20,000 feet the champagne blew up and froze the bomb bay doors shut so we could not jettison the contraband. The juice was just melting when we taxied to our hardstand much to the joy of the ground crew who held mess kits under the drain tubes. The Colonel's ship had the same problems, but he should have known better!

John McLane recalled his memories of the air ground echelon:

One could get the impression by reading the record of the 8th Air Force that only the flying officers and men were responsible for the tremendous damage done to Hitler's Europe. Nothing could be further from the truth. Without the ground support personnel, not one bomber could ever have flown. I read with great interest Will Lundy's description of the April 14th, 1945 'Salute to the Ground Men Weeks' event where 600 ground men gathered at the main ramp to be lauded by Gen Leon Johnson and Colonel Snavely. General Johnson, standing on the spot where he himself had received the Congressional Medal of Honour, stressed that for every aircraft in the air, 90 ground men each did his thing to make it possible. I wish I had been there to add my praise and shake as many hands as possible.

Will Lundy was an assistant ground crew chief with the 44th Bomb Group and became the group's historian. He provided a vivid account of his life as a B24 mechanic:

The first winter out on the 'line' was very difficult and terribly demanding. Our only shelter from the biting cold, rain or snow and even darkness was our plane itself or the weapon-carrier left by the combat crew. Of course, the plane had no heating system for us nor did she have lighting other than the instrument lights in the cockpit . . . All maintenance or repairs performed in the early morning hours or at night had to be done by flashlight. No electric lights, ever. This same work could seldom be accomplished wearing gloves, especially working in the engine nacelle or accessory sections. So much of the time it was bare-handed work in freezing weather and one could only continue as long as he could feel the wrench in his hand, then someone else must take over while you somehow managed to work some feeling back into your frozen digits. There was no structures of buildings with heat close by, no line shacks, nothing – no place with a fire in which to warm up. And, of course, no open fires were permitted or advisable during blackouts. My remedy was to don my gloves and run up and down the taxiway, slapping my hands together – literally beating the circulation back into my fingers.

Vernon Ellis remembered how difficult it was to work with cold hands:

When your fingers were so cold it was difficult sometimes to tell if they were grasping anything or not, so we had to be extra careful that we did not drop anything down inside the engine or some critical areas of the aircraft. Of course we did drop nuts, bolts, washers etc., on rare occasions. It was inevitable with numb fingers. But when this happened it usually meant an additional two or three hours work to remove it. We didn't dare leave it rattling around loose where it could jam a control rod, pulley, cable or short out some electrical system. Sometimes it took an hour to find the object with only a flash light to work with and often it was unreachable after you had located it. We could sometimes retrieve it with a long handled magnet, a piece of wire or as a last resort we could dismantle several components of the aeroplane to reach it. Dropping an item down into the 'workings' of an aeroplane was a disaster.

Aeroplane mechanics mainly had to work outside all year round because most bases only had one or two hangars. Vernon recalled:

It's hard to explain to anyone who did not have the responsibility for an aircraft just how much the aircraft dominated your life. After a while, it became the only reason for your existence. You were both its master and slave. Seven days a week you cleaned, adjusted, serviced, babied, cursed, nursed and fixed it. During the winter months you rarely saw it in daylight. Take off was before dawn and it returned after dark so all your work was done with the aid of a flashlight! On days when there was no flying, it was usually because the weather was bad, so any work had to be done in the rain. We became like a bunch of grooms caring for a thoroughbred racehorse, or pages preparing a knight and his horse for battle! No matter where we went, the condition of the aircraft was always in the back of our minds. I can recall numerous times when one of the men would return from leave, or a three day pass and the first thing he would say was 'How's the ship'. We were possessed by it.

We were constantly looking at the aeroplane, looking for worn tires, fuel leaks, cracks, or previously undetected flack holes. We even gave the engines a good check out, even after a successful mission when the crew reported that everything was OK. Quite often we would find something wrong. Maybe 150rpm mag drop on No. 4, a generator burned out on No. 2, a sluggish prop governor on No. 1, or a tire with a bad spot, maybe a couple of small flack holes that the flight crew had not even felt. At any rate, we became pessimists, always looking for trouble and being ill at ease if we didn't find any. After many months on the same aircraft, you became so familiar with it that you knew every scratch, dent or peculiarity of each access panel. Some went back on easy, while others had to be twisted in a precise manner or they didn't fit properly.

When a plane was lost it was only a day or so until we had a spanking brand new one. One would think this would be a pleasant occasion, but it wasn't. We all had a tendency to resent this recruit interloper stepping into the shoes of our old friend who had recently 'died' in combat. We would approach this new 'bird' cautiously and with some reluctance. Who was this upstart with no dents or scratches, smelling of new paint and preening like a peacock.

Some of the older aircrews were reluctant to fly a new aircraft on its first combat mission. Here was an untried entity with no combat record, no experience over enemy territory. Hell, the guns had never been fired! How will it do in a tight situation? I'll fly the damn thing, but I'd prefer an old one with some kind of reputation. I think my pilots felt also that it was like they were taking a virgin out to be gang raped!

The line shack was considered a 'life saver' by Vernon who recalled that his was so comfortable that some of the men rarely went back to the barracks. There were practical benefits too because the dispersal areas for the aeroplanes were often several miles from the living quarters. The shacks were not official buildings, but retreats from the weather built from anything that could be scrounged or improvised. Ground crews worked as a team and the line shacks provided them with a private and enclosed area in which to work on smaller aircraft components without being exposed to the elements unnecessarily.

AMERICAN RED CROSS CLUBMOBILE, 44TH BOMB GROUP, SHIPDHAM. *(Will Lundy)*

The American Red Cross provided a refreshment service to the ground crews, known as the Clubmobile, although some ground personnel could not recall ever having seen one. They took coffee and doughnuts out to the men in the dispersal areas, thereby reassuring them that they were not forgotten. The girls who ran the Clubmobile always took time out to chat with the men.

Endorsements of the dedication and excellence of ground personnel can be found throughout any history of the Air Forces – they were the first to arrive and the last to leave. They may never have shone in the way the airmen did, but they were always there working hard and their contribution was widely acknowledged to be of incalculable value.

8

The Importance of Morale and Health

Morale is the capacity to stay on the job – especially a long, hard job – with determination and zest. It is the opposite of apathy.

PSYCHOLOGY FOR THE FIGHTING MAN (1943)

Army commanders generally had a very good understanding of the negative effects of low morale and most went to some lengths to ensure healthy mental and physical working conditions for their men. However, policy-making in this regard was hampered by the fact that the bomb groups were living in a war zone and that decisions were instigated by officials back in the USA who might never have even visited an air base in Britain.

Morale could be influenced at group level, especially by such things as casualties and combat losses (often massaged or suppressed by the authorities for this very reason) or successes. Poor food had a detrimental effect on everyone, although food on the American air bases was reportedly quite good. More interesting fare was often made available for various festivals and other celebrations.

To each individual, the factors surrounding his own state of morale were complex. He might have had concerns about his home and family and his limited contact with them or been preoccupied with how much longer it would be before he could return. He could also have been disturbed by the loss or injury of friends in combat. More positively, spirits could be lifted by mail from home and romantic liaisons (at least for as long as they were successful).

C.O. Charles Dougher at the new officers' club, 94th Bomb Group, Rougham. *(Frank Halm)*

The morale-boosting value of songs was something that had been appreciated by the military for a long time. In World War 1, the song 'Over There' had been very popular. The USAAF devised their own anthem 'Off We Go into the Wild Blue Yonder' but some bomb groups even had their own ones. However, air crews did not sing as they took off for a mission. Frank Halm remembered that this was an extremely noisy time and crews could only speak with each other through microphones and earphones if they had something important to say:

> *Chatter was forbidden. This was no time or place for fun and games. OK after we were parked and shut down.*

Take off was a very stressful time for bomber crews; the bomb bay was loaded and they did not know whether they would return in good condition, or at all. Therefore, the only noise was that of the aircraft engines, which was very loud. Frank remembered that they sometimes sang 'Off we go into the Wild Blue Yonder' at the Officer's Club 'when most of us were a bit under the influence'.

Entertainment was provided by Special Services personnel, or by anyone else they could recruit. Bob Hope made many trips to Britain to entertain the servicemen and it was remembered that he was very good at raising morale.

The Hollywood actors James Stewart and Clark Gable had both volunteered for combat duty and were posted to England. Those who met them felt very strongly that their presence was an aid to morale, as they mixed very well with all the men.

GI ARTWORK IN NISSEN HUT AT 361ST FIGHTER GROUP, BOTTISHAM, 1986. *(Tony Stuart)*

That there were clearly some very competent artists among the Americans who came to Britain is demonstrated by the artwork they made in their huts. These pieces of work include pretty girls and scenes from home.

Good physical and mental health were of vital importance but could be difficult to maintain in wartime England. The men would have arrived into the UK in tip-top condition, but conditions there often eroded their good health and sense of well being.

Long working hours and lack of sleep are features of any war zone, although the men of the Army Air Forces were better off than the average infantry soldier in that they did have beds to retire to as opposed to snatching short bursts of sleep whilst squatting in a foxhole. Even so, one bombardier recalled that 'sleep was precious'. Crews designated for combat needed to be woken in the small hours of the morning by the Charge of Quarters Sergeant, and John Bright (CQ ser-

DINAH SHORE ARRIVING AT 94TH BOMB GROUP, ROUGHAM, 200 MISSION PARTY. *(Frank Halm)*

geant) recalled that they were often heard grunting and swearing as they dragged themselves out of their beds and set about preparing for the day. Those who survived their missions returned exhausted some time during the late afternoon. After debriefing and a meal if they wished, they could retire to bed, but many were not sufficiently relaxed and able to sleep. With their GI neighbours coming and going and noises from the base at work, some needed to unwind at the bar, or with friends. Bob Banta remembered the disturbance of occasional Luftwaffe raids on their field in 1943, but it was not always the enemy that kept him awake.

> *The noise of the planes having their engines checked out by running them up to a high rpm was usually enough to keep us awake. We played cards until we could fall asleep. I would guess that I averaged about two hours or less of sleep per night. I always slept for long periods of time immediately after returning from a raid. We all did. We slept while we were 'forming up' into battle formation which usually took one or two hours before we headed for Germany.*

Al Jones slept badly for other reasons:

> *I slept below our co-pilot who was a chain smoker – I'd often wake up to ash streaming down from above and choking with smoke. I would also lay awake listening to the RAF overhead.*

Ground staff had their own sleep problems, especially those in constant contact with the combat aeroplanes. A crew chief noted in his diary the erratic sleeping hours he had to contend with:

> *Worked all day and until midnight repairing battle damage and replacing an engine . . . Got up at 4.15am (in December) to pre-flight . . . They had us up 3 times during the night as someone had a brainstorm and wanted #846 to fly next day . . . We slept until noon . . . as it was, we worked until 3.30am until we finished the job.*

An entry for the following February (1944) notes: 'Payday – slept all day.'

It was often difficult to express the extent of the exhaustion felt to those at home and Jim Sheller was almost apologetic in a letter to his wife. 'I suppose this is getting monotonous for you my saying how tired I am and how I don't feel like writing much'. However, even under these circumstances, his letters were not without humour:

> *Some program I have, out of the sack and into the flack, out of the flack*

and back to the sack and out of the sack and back to the flack . . . mumble
mummmble . . . combat don't bother me none, me none, meeenonne . . .

Combat flying sapped both physical and mental energy and Bert Stiles recorded that after his first mission:

I was so shot I didn't want to move. My flying had been lousy. My hair
was spongy with sweat and my eyes felt like they'd been sanded down and
wrapped in a dry sack.

After twelve days and eight more missions:

We were like old men. It seemed like the sun had gone out of the world. I
looked in the mirror and a haggard mask of a face stared back at me.

Bert Stiles was so tired at one stage that he 'felt drunk'. He became rather obsessive about sleep and even fantasised about his bed of the future:

Some day I'm going to have a bed of my own design. It will be 12 foot in
diameter and it will be perfectly round with a deep inner spring mattress
built to fit. I'll be able to get into it from any direction from any angle. And
right into the middle, in the softest part, there'll be a girl.

During time off sleep was high on the list of priorities and it was not unknown for leave to be used for the purpose of catching up on lost sleep. Some combat men even slept through evening mess on returning from combat. This exhaustion, coupled with the anxiety of combat itself, led to the weight loss which was noted by many at the time. A gunner lost 20 lb in seven months, which he blamed on poor eating habits, 12–14 hour missions and 'K' rations (food to eat while flying) which he could not ingest through an oxygen mask. Too exhausted to eat, he usually went straight to bed after debriefing.

Lack of sleep made men more susceptible to disease. The common cold became debilitating and on one base men actually boasted about the severity of their particular cold and how long it lasted. Colds were blamed on the British winter, but it was more likely that the men had lowered immunity if they were in a poor physical condition. With their long working hours and lack of rest, secondary infections such as sinus problems and coughs were commonplace. Combat men with colds were automatically grounded because the change in pressure caused pain in the sinuses. A gunner who managed to go into battle with a cold said that 'at altitude it felt like someone had planted a hatchet between my eyes'.

Dr Earl Kopeke, a Flight Surgeon, remembered that the drug Sulphona-mide, a precursor of antibiotics, was seen as a prophylactic treatment for many conditions including colds. Apparently, men were encouraged to take this in tablet form in an attempt to remain healthy. There was, of course, no way to prevent the cold virus being transmitted from one person to another in a confined space, so not only was it ineffective, but some people were said to have been allergic to this preparation and developed skin rashes. Earl also recalled that although penicillin, the first antibiotic, was invented in 1929, it took many years for this to be satisfactorily manufactured. There were not enough supplies to treat every injured soldier until 1944.

Scabies was a fairly common skin condition which was also infectious. Caused by a tiny mite which lived in dirty beds and bedding, it caused itching and soreness of the skin, sometimes resulting in infections. It was virtually impossible to maintain high standards of hygiene on any air base because of the long working hours. Some bases had non-existent or very poor bathing facilities. Washing bedding would not have been easy and woollen blankets provided an ideal environment for these mites. Some men also recollected a shortage of sheets for their beds and that blankets went unlaundered for the duration of the war.

Crab lice (a genital problem) also thrived in the close living conditions and again, dirty beds assisted in their transmission as did sexual inter-course with some British girls, particularly prostitutes.

Among the most dominant, widespread and serious conditions which had to be dealt with were the venereal diseases. A pilot recalled:

V D lectures and films back at the base were frightening and usually more than enough to curtail one's lust for 48 hours!

Dick Carboneau recalled the time when one of the monthly squadron briefings culminated with a 'Prizegiving':

On one occasion we were informed that the 322nd had won the 'Iron Cross', a back-handed award given to the squadron with the highest venereal disease rate. An oversized sheet aluminium replica of an Iron Cross had to hang on our headquarters wall until another squadron 'won' it.

These films and lectures often centred on the fact that venereal diseases were difficult and often painful to treat. It could well be that films of these horrendous treatments were shown on base with the intention of making the condition as fearful as possible.

VD was considered to be a self-inflicted disease and the Army Air Force showed little sympathy for the sufferers. They were treated with the best methods available at the time, but were subsequently demoted and (if they were fliers) automatically grounded. One Bomb Group Commander regularly withdrew passes for the whole company if there was an increase in VD among his men. On another base, prophylactic kits were issued to every man as he boarded the truck to Norwich and one recipient remembered:

> Our Catholic chaplain objected to this, so he transferred out. You either took it, or got off the truck. There must be thousands of them lining the ditches into Norwich.

Naturally good health was essential to the smooth working of the base and to morale generally, but aviators were particularly sensitive about it because if they were grounded, they lost momentum in combat. Periods of sickness protracted their stay in Britain and they would find themselves waving goodbye to their regular crew who had completed their missions. They would then have to complete their number of missions with a different crew which many found rather a disquieting prospect. Consequently many men went into combat feeling under the weather to avoid being grounded. Combat in itself sometimes caused health issues and a flier remembered that he was often constipated because 'at altitude it was too cold to use the pot'. Another remembers arriving back at the base every time with a splitting headache.

Jim McMahon recalled that

> the matter of body gas was important because the higher we flew the more gas bubbles would expand. At some altitudes expansion could be as much as ten times the amount at sea level. We can assume this is why they never fed us a pot of beans before a mission!

Several bases recorded instances of food poisoning and John McLane wrote that one evening

> I, along with other combat officers, ate at our Combat Officers' Mess. We had not been back in the squadron long before I began to feel faint. I was the first to become sick, so I got a lot of attention. Medics were called in, as I was violently ill. They rushed me to the base hospital where I was the first to be admitted . . . The special attention did not last long as the hospital quickly filled to overflow capacity. Dozens of flying officers began to arrive and soon there was no place to put them except on the floor. They were all as sick as myself and complete bedlam and pandemonium broke loose . . . I

*did not know it at the time but we had contracted Ptomaine poisoning from
a certain pie served for dessert . . . As a result of so many combat officers
being stricken and the severity of the illness, the missions of the 24th and
25th were scrubbed.*

This was the first of three such incidents for this particular man.

Many cases of diarrhoea were recorded among flying personnel whilst in
the air – no doubt the result of stress.

Homesickness, though not really a medical problem, was difficult to
remedy because the only real option was to send the soldier home. Earl
Rudolph recalled his Christmas in England:

*We had radios in our rooms at the base and we were listening to Bing Crosby
sing 'White Christmas' at home in the news.*

The newspapers reported on race riots, zoot suits, persecution in California
and rather silly songs such as 'Maizy Dotes' sweeping the land. He felt that
America was changing while he was away and that

*it would not be the same place that we knew and loved . . . With every
week of our separation from home the longing grew, that was not merely
homesickness, but a feeling of exile and loss of touch.*

During the cold winter of 1943, Dan O'Keefe found that snowball fights
made him melancholy with thoughts of home, and a first reveille after two
months away struck a chord for some:

*After the ceremony, there was no talking, we just looked at each other and
walked back into the barracks, lay down on our beds feeling homesick. The
sight of our flag had brought thoughts of home to each of us.*

Mail from home was essential for maintaining morale and it was a vital link
to all that the men were familiar with. Servicemen were provided with an
official air letter known as 'V' mail which carried the franking privilege and
was photographically reduced so as to take up less space. The Army did its
best to keep a good mail link going, but it did not always arrive when it
should, as noted by Jim Sheller in a letter home to his wife:

*Got your letter of April 17th today, a day after the one mailed on the 21st,
so sequence means nothing . . . Your mail is coming through in about 12–20
days . . . Darling, your exhilarating letters help muchly.*

And, in a diary note, in June 1944:

MAIL TRUCK ARRIVING AT 93RD BOMB GROUP, HARDWICK. *(Jim McMahon)*

Five days since any of us has received any mail. Apparently, shipping space is too short.

All outgoing letters from enlisted men had to be censored by officers. Censor duty was not generally popular with these officers because they felt they were prying into men's private thoughts. Some felt that officers' mail should also have been censored. Privileged information could still be got home in other ways. One man told his wife to take eight away from his age and that was how many missions he still had to do. Another man was more overt and sent a letter home to his mother via a friend who was going back to the USA. This letter, written in March 1944, began: 'I will now give you some information that I don't want you to pass onto anyone but Rita' (his sister). It goes on to describe his various missions, with dates and numbers of aircraft shot down. This letter came after a particularly bad mission and he described to his parents his innermost feelings:

All at once I was knocked down as something hit me in the back. A piece of flack was sticking out of my jacket. I was so scared by now that I could hardly stand up and I couldn't see as the sweat was running into my eyes. The temperature was 45 degrees below too. Well, we went into a crazy spin, and I was half way out of the window when the pilot pulled it out and we headed for home. We almost didn't make it . . . After this raid my nerves were so shot I could hardly write . . . It is the most terrible experience you can have . . . I saw two ships blow up this day and another go down by fighters.

Of course, this is exactly the kind of morale-destroying and militarily sensitive information that the Army did not want to leak out.

Parcels from home were particularly appreciated and seen as a piece of America sent to England. Jim Sheller wrote a thank you letter to his wife in 1944:

Received my request package honey, really was a welcome sight, not so much for the content as the fact that your own little hands put so much loving care into it . . . Could you send me some unpopped corn. It's a real treat when we fix it up after a long day.

However, these gifts were often badly packed and subjected to rough handling in transit. One ground crewman remembered that they were 'most welcome if you enjoyed powdered cookies'. In addition they often took a long time to arrive.

One mother sent her son a parcel of bananas. They were a mess when they arrived, but the combat man remembered that 'she meant well'. A friend of his received baloney sausage from home. 'He shared it and it was a real treat.' American newspapers were always appreciated, especially the local rags which told of friends at home. Naturally, these were well out of date by the time they reached their destination.

One thing the Air Force had no control over was the contents of incoming mail. Perhaps the most devastating of all wartime mail was the 'Dear John' letter where the wife or sweetheart told the soldier that she had found another man. These were far too common among the men of the USAAF and one ground crew man remembered that in his hut of 36 men, 14 received such letters. He himself was a very young married man and when he heard that his wife had left him, he developed a drink problem which necessitated him attending the base hospital for treatment.

Bob Banta described his feelings when trying to answer a 'Dear John' letter:

One heard about others getting them, but now I knew first hand how they can hurt. Having a lovely girl to talk and dream about was one of the few joys left in this war. Now it was gone. Other airmen of the two crews in the hut straggled in from the mess and sat about discussing a variety of subjects. I sat cross-legged on the bunk with the letter. Only two lines had been written.

Between the catchy conversation and my own rambling thoughts, progress was slow. Anyway, what could I say?

The keeping of animals, particularly dogs, played a large part in the relief of loneliness and, for many, fulfilled the desire for affection with no strings attached. Responsibility for these animals was accepted by individuals or a whole squadron and the animals were fed on mess hall scraps. Some were picked up as strays, but one gunner was given a puppy by his girlfriend. After the animal wet on his bed, he said he 'pitched it out of the hut forever' where it was no doubt adopted by another Yank.

For many, the keeping of a dog – a constant figure in an uncertain and dangerous world – was established earlier by the Battle of Britain pilots. However, ground personnel also kept dogs, mainly to ease their loneliness and to have

CHARGE OF QUARTERS SERGEANT JOHN BRIGHT WITH HIS PET DOG. 95TH BOMB GROUP, HORHAM. *(John Bright)*

something of their own to care for and to nurture. John Bright, a Charge of Quarters sergeant who was in England for a considerable time, remembered his attachment to his dog:

I had a pet dog which I kept in my Nissen Hut. One man in the hut wanted the dog out, but I replied that it was my pet and it was staying. A rather heated argument ensued and one of our men advised our adjutant who promptly moved the man to another hut. None of the men in my quarters liked him – we all preferred the dog!

Some dogs lived exceedingly good lives on base and many became group mascots. One such animal has gone down in the history of the 94th Bomb Group:

A beloved member of the 94th at Rougham was Toby, an Alsatian dog . . . Toby became acquainted with everyone on base, but he was alleged to be rank

GIs WITH PET GOAT. 95TH BOMB GROUP, HORHAM. *(John Bright)*

happy. It wasn't that he preferred pinks and green, or plush officer's clubs so much that he loved to ride in a jeep. And he seems to have figured out that officers were more likely to have access to such luxury. His master went home and he became attached to a flying officer who took him to France. Toby would sit in the back of Frank's jeep in total ecstasy as he made his round on the base and in the local community.

Frank concluded that 'Toby was known by everyone, was a part of the 94th legacy and a grand dog.'

In the absence of the strict quarantine laws of today, animals were often brought into England from foreign countries. GIs who had been in North Africa sometimes brought exotic birds and monkeys, although all too often these had a short life because the owners lacked the knowledge of how to care for them properly. However, one Company Commander successfully looked after a honey bear.

There are some reports of dogs actually being taken into combat, although these could only have been at low altitude, or the dogs would have died of lack of oxygen. One dog, according to Bert Stiles, was taken on a milk run to France, but after a while he became 'flack-happy' and tried to jump out of the window.

An unofficial way of maintaining morale in any group was the incessant horseplay among the men. This was mostly good humoured and well intended, but it did occasionally get out of hand. 'Buzzing' the base or a friend's house was a favourite, but this was dangerous and strictly against the rules. Bob Banta remembered buzzing the local fighter base on return from his crew's final mission. His pilot put the Fortress into a huge dive:

My heart pounded with concern because I knew we didn't have much room for such a manoeuvre. He [the pilot] finally pulled up on the deck of an airfield that I hadn't been able to see. Only then did I realise he was buzzing the base of the fighter that so often plagued us. Oh, how we scattered those clods! It made me so happy that I yelled and banged the desk for more!

A B17 pilot admitted that he would surreptitiously stop the watches of the other officers in the hut, just to enjoy the confusion. One group went onto a farm and played American football with small haystacks, scattering the hay far and wide. This was a thoughtless thing to do and needless to say the farmer did not see the funny side.

Jim McMahon clearly recalled an incident after a few drinks in his rest home in Southport:

A few others and I were heading back to our hotel and 'goosing imaginary butterflies'. We were walking along and parallel to the beach when Lo! Wot 'av we 'ere? A giant cement flowerpot next to the steps leading to the boardwalk. We immediately liberated it and were quite well on our way to the hotel when out of the darkness came an authoritative voice asking 'Wot's goin' on 'ere?' A tall Bobby appeared and directed us to return the travelling pot to the place from where we had liberated it. He came along to see that we did not shirk our responsibility to the pot. When it was restored to its original place next to the steps, he tipped his hat, thanked us and disappeared again. I will always remember that workout and his courtesy. I don't think the incident went into his book.

These pranksters were not always mindful of rank. Dan O'Keefe remembered that on one occasion a condom was filled with water and the face of the barracks chief painted on it. The item was hung from the ceiling on the Nissen hut between the double doors. A participant in the joke recalled that 'when the inspecting officer saw it, he folded up with laughter'.

Target Germany, a booklet produced in 1944 by the US Army Air Forces, tells how the men teased each other constantly:

> *In the mess one day a pilot got up disgustedly, complaining that the navigators talked too much shop. The navigators, in a huff, said they would organise a table and eat by themselves. 'Well' said the pilot with a wicked grin, 'see that you have it near the door; otherwise you guys'll never find it.'*

Close friendships between the men themselves did much to keep up morale. Many combat crews were extremely close and some even owed one another their lives. Because crews operated as a team in the air, their sense of responsibility toward each other was hard to lay aside and often manifested itself in social situations from covering up a friend's absence on base to putting him to bed if he had drunk too much.

Rank consciousness evaporated in the close brotherhood of a combat crew, although opinions differed as to whether such closeness was always a good thing. One gunner preferred to fly with the crews he did not know too well because he found it easier to accept the possibility of their deaths or his own death if he was not close to them. The majority of combat men however, needed and responded to this unique relationship with their crews. Redding and Leyshon's *Skyways to Berlin* (1944) noted the experience of a Captain Spain who replaced a pilot who had been killed. Sent straight into battle, he was very uneasy at not having had the chance to get to know his crew:

> *I hustled over to the briefing room where I met the navigator and bombardier of my crew for the first time. We exchanged polite greetings, too damned polite. I could feel them eyeing me up and I guess I was giving them the Double O too. But we were polite, very damned polite about it all.*

The mission was postponed for a few hours

> *which gave me the opportunity to meet the rest of the crew. We got together and I made a point of wanting to inspect the ship. What I really wanted to do was to improve my time with those 9 guys. They had flown together a long time and they called each other by their first names and to hell with rank as good crews do. But to them I was Captain Spain, or plain 'Sir'. They'd never heard of a guy called Bill. After take off I was concerned about the careful GI response I was getting on the intercom whenever I checked gun situations, or asked about position or altitude. They were tossing back the 'sirs' that just don't belong in a bomber after she's airborne.*

A story in the same book stated that Captain Spain flew excellent evasive action from flack and fighters. On the way back a crewmember called him 'skipper' which he admitted 'warmed him all over'. They were attacked and the bomber was shot up enough to necessitate bailing out, but they decided to stick it out and try to make for home. With failing brakes, they overshot the runway and landed in a field, luckily with no casualties. Captain Spain noted that by this time he was 'Bill'.

John McLane's manuscript tells the story of four enlisted men who got drunk on Vitalis hair tonic. They ran into the officers' hut on all fours barking like dogs. One even had a leash around his neck. They ran riot in the officers' hut jumping up on the bunks and generally creating havoc. The officers would have been well within their rights to take disciplinary action, but John explained:

> Luckily there was no mission scheduled for us the next day because I'm sure that at least four of our crew would have never made it. One might ask why were enlisted men allowed to take such liberties with their officers. To understand that would be to realise the camaraderie that existed among the members of a flying crew.

Unfortunately, not all relationships were so straightforward. Bert Stiles had noted after his first mission that he only wanted to be with his crew, but after several missions:

> A great crew is just about as rare a thing as a football team. They just come along once in a while. There isn't much you can do about it if you're not I guess. It's a spontaneous thing . . . Somehow we didn't have it.

It is interesting that the pilot requested Stiles' removal from the crew and that they went on to successfully finish their tours of duty separately. After a particularly rough mission with his second crew in a state of emotional turmoil, Bert wanted to tell his pilot 'that I was glad I was on his crew, and that it was the best goddam crew I'd ever heard of'.

One popular way of relieving tension was sport and all the bases organised basketball and American football games. These were also good for the men's general health. Not all sporting events were confined to the American bases, however. The magazine *Norfolk Fair* published an article in 1977 pointing out that baseball games had been played at Carrow Road (the Norwich City football ground) during the war and that there was even a Wild West Show there in 1944.

Al Jones never forgot his time on the Norwich golf course. He remembered:

I played golf twice on the Norwich course which had been ploughed up (presumably for growing food) except for seven holes. On my second visit, I had with me three new golf balls that I had brought from the USA. A British golfer nearby saw these and really drooled as he had not seen a new golf ball in years. After I had finished playing I gave him the three balls. I thought he was going to kiss me.

Among the more useful morale builders were the medals handed out to fliers. Frank Halm received an Air Medal after his fifth mission and received an Oak Leaf Cluster after every further five missions. He also received the Distinguished Flying Cross which was well above the Air Medal. It was awarded for a special achievement and he was cited for 13 particular missions. Other fliers who performed heroic deeds had to be awarded the medal posthumously. However, not all combat men welcomed these medals in the spirit which they were intended, and in this the Air Medal was a major casualty. Bert Stiles was derisory:

Air Medals come in boxes. They are sent to each squadron by the medal department of the Army which is a hardworking outfit. Whenever the boxes begin to clog up the works there is a presentation.

Dick Carboneau, a recipient of the Air Medal, remembered:

There were squadron briefings perhaps once a month. Air Medal citations were handed out here. We called them 'hero slips' and treated them as a kind of joke. Every aircrew member received the Air Medal for flying 5 missions and an oak leaf cluster signifying a repeat award for each 5 thereafter. A gunner could have slept through 5 missions and still won it. Our Pilot called it 'the Air Mattress with Barbed wire Clusters'. As far as we were concerned those little mimeographed slips were just certificates acknowledging survival of 5 more missions. Their greatest value became evident after the end of the war, when we found that they were coupons towards earlier discharge.

Military decorations – honours earned in battle – were considered much more precious. Missions that had to be aborted for reasons of bad weather or mechanical failure were particularly damaging to morale. Obviously, aborts wasted the time and effort of the ground support staff, who had to wake up early to prepare the aeroplanes for missions. Most of all it affected the crew members who had been psychologically prepared to do battle that day. Stiles took off for Germany in an older bomber which the pilot termed 'a crate'. The crew was lined up for a 'rough mission', but the pilot decided to abort when the plane lost altitude and speed and had oxygen pressure problems. They had never aborted before, and Stiles noted that he felt 'pretty fed up' even though the ground crew chief subsequently assured him that they would never have made it to Germany.

> *I knew what they were all thinking. No guts. A rough one, so they come home . . . Nobody looked at anyone else while we unloaded our stuff. Nobody made much noise. The sun shone wanly through the mist . . . I felt as beat-up as if we'd gone all the way.*

Target Germany made much of the stress caused by missions which were called off at the last minute.

> *Combat crews declared, almost unanimously, that the feeling of let-down, the sense of anticlimax that followed these cancellations was far worse than actual participation in a combat fight. The strain of sitting through a briefing, or enduring those stomach-tightening minutes of tension before take-off, the uncertainty of being told to stand by for an indefinite period of time, the final 'scrubbing' – these things left the crews so limp that one group commander sent in a formal request to have diversionary sweeps credited to fliers as combat missions. The request was refused, but it indicated the seriousness of the problem. In the month of December alone such 'scrubbings' occurred seven different times. And when they happened the ground crews which had loaded the bombs and groomed the bombers felt almost as defeated as the fighting men.*

Rather strangely, there was a certain amount of resentment directed towards non-flying officers. West Point was the ultimate in officer training, but with such a large volume of officers needed in a war, some went to courses at Officer's Candidate School (OCS) for a three month training programme, otherwise known as '90 day wonders'. Forty years after the war, a veteran gunner still felt that these officers 'seemed to excel mainly in arrogance'.

It is unfortunate, yet fascinating, that it was the non-flying officers who were the least favourably remembered. Some stories which are recalled reveal the antipathy some men felt all that time ago and Al Jones spoke of

> *the saluting demons with their petty little gripes and 'by the book' behaviour which did not fit into a war zone where your friends were being shot up and your neck possibly on the line next.*

> *We had a first class group commander who was returned to the USA and got*

in his place a poor replacement who had failed already with another group which had to be disbanded. His second and third he brought with him and were soon nicknamed 'The Brain' and 'The Skull'. Both were contemptuous of lower ranks, but particularly fliers.

In another instance, Dan O'Keefe recalled the time when his Squadron Commander (a flying officer) and his executive (a ground officer) crash-landed while on a local flight:

I was visiting a friend in hospital when I noticed the executive officer wearing his Major's oak leaves pinned on to the lapels of his hospital GI robe. I felt that was unnecessary. We all knew who he was!

Feelings were particularly vehement towards Air Intelligence Officers who, according to the fliers, appeared to be out of touch with reality. A navigator admitted he had no respect for them:

I (and many other flying crew members) particularly loathed the mess officers, intelligence officers, morale officers and their ilk who outranked us heavily and lived extremely well. We particularly disliked the intelligence officers who superciliously conducted debriefings on the premise that we were supposed to have seen what they, in their wisdom, said we would see. They did not want any reports given to them unless they completely agreed with the pre-determined facts. The fact that few if any of them ever dared fly on a mission added to our feelings of disgust. In my particular bombardment group, the high placed flying officers (Commanding Officer, Executive Officer, Group Bombardier, Group Navigator etc.) rarely, if ever, flew on a combat mission. Yes, also, I consider that the ground officers received better treatment, better food and without doubt had a pleasant life goading the fliers onto total victory, so to speak.

Dan O'Keefe agreed:

Intelligence Officers were very standoffish. They were 'cold fish', concerned with target photos and detailed locations of where the planes went down. I usually just sat and stared at them. They were very sceptical of whatever we said.

The alleged insensitivity of Intelligence Officers is further borne out by the famous feature film *Twelve o'Clock High*. Following a disastrous mission, the debriefing officer is portrayed as a man eager to obtain information, but un-impressed by, even uncaring about, what the men had just been through.

For many veterans feelings ran high on this subject, but it could be that after life-threatening combat men were physically and emotionally drained and in no mood to be questioned about anything.

In his book *Elusive Horizons* Keith Schuyler wrote that a friend of his was pleased because a particular paddlefoot major had suffered food poisoning after eating several pieces of Boston Cream Pie and was still in hospital the next day:

> *I shared Jack's pleasure. No one could satisfactorily explain why the rank of Major seemed to settle upon every crummy bastard in the Army. There were fine Majors, especially among the flying officers, but the paddlefeet with the gold oak leaf seemed to fit into a class all their own.*

Bert Stiles arrived at a pre-briefing breakfast on 'D' Day at 1 a.m. where 'all the rank in the group made chow, tables full of majors and colonels and captains'. A crewmember joked about there being a late bridge party, and someone else said: 'ground gripping bastards. They go to bed when we get up.'

Added to this, there was a strong suspicion that non-flying officers ate better and lived better, although this is difficult to confirm. Once a rumour began, it gained momentum as seeds of discontent fell on very fertile ground. It may be that the ground officers had the incentive to provide themselves with more comfortable surroundings, as they were in England for longer. There is certainly no hard evidence to suggest that they ate different food from that of the flying officers. One man recalled that the ground officers on his base had white tablecloths, whereas the flying officers ate from wooden tables. Such differences may now seem trivial, but would have added to the general feeling of resentment.

There was certainly a feeling of distrust, even contempt, between the flyers and the ground officers. Aviators, who lived dangerously, were irritated by seemingly unnecessary rules and restrictions. On the base for a short time and constantly flouting authority, flying officers often behaved as 'one of the boys', getting drunk in the presence of enlisted men and breaking all the rules of rank, especially when in the company of their own crew members. Combat men received more pay, but felt that it was more difficult to obtain promotion.

From the perspective of the ground officer, the fliers were sometimes seen as 'spoilt heroes'. Nevertheless, no doubt they were highly conscious that the combat men were risking their lives daily whilst they themselves remained safe on the ground. It was the ground officers who had to send these men to their deaths, often feeling that the importance of their own jobs went unrecognised. Their public arrogance, therefore, could have been a buffer against their perceived lack of status. It is also likely that airmen took more liberties secure in the knowledge that they were a much-needed commodity. Elmer Bendiner relates the story of a bed requisitioned by one of his gunners and obviously meant for a 'paddlefoot lieutenant'.

One Sunday morning, three weeks before Schweinfurt [a massive bombing mission], the adjutant on inspection, came to Mike's barracks. He was a beefy, paddlefoot lieutenant who, it was said, deserved an embarrassment medal because he suffered so from the disorderly presence of combat soldiers, they upset his schedule and affronted his dignity . . . He came to Mike's magnificent bed. It was a Hollywood bed – a wooden frame on which rested a box spring surrounded with a mattress that was gentle but firm. Alongside the humdrum GI cots it stood majestic as a fourposter . . . the colonel towered over the little gunner, but gunners were in short supply. 'I see you're sleeping well sergeant' said the colonel . . . we rehearsed yet again Mike's triumph.

John Bright, a CQ sergeant whose job involved waking up the combat crews for their missions, felt that far less fuss was made by a flying officer if asked to censor a letter home. When John was given a shot pheasant by some British friends, he shared it with three combat officers, who in turn, brought iced ale from their mess to share with him. The sergeant was also flown to Edinburgh for two days by some flying officers who 'okayed it' with his superior. John also recalled a pleasant incident involving a non-combat officer.

I remember one day the Captain asked if I would help paint the orderly room. He was expecting some inspectors. The Captain and I painted it and finished around 1 am. He asked if I was hungry. He took the jeep and went to the mess hall and returned with bread, butter, a chunk of roast beef and three cans of peaches. We ate the beef and opened one of the tins. The other two he gave to me.

Stories of rank were not without their humorous moments. The 44th Bomb Group history tells of an officer on a bicycle who was saluted by a private. The officer attempted to return the salute, but fell off the bike and into the canal. Next morning the group bulletin board proclaimed that no longer should officers be saluted when riding bikes!

On another occasion a B26 navigator remembered the night when the siren went off and everyone ran to the air raid shelter.

Our operations officer slipped and fell one night and was trampled on crying 'You can't do this to me. I'm a Major'. He was the last one in!

John McLane particularly enjoyed the revelry of his 200th mission party at the 44th Bomb Group at Shipdham when 'rank' lost its privileges on this day of fun. No one was allowed to display his rank and defaulters would be thrown in the duck pond on base:

I could not believe my eyes when I saw a group of men grab Col. John Gibson who was dressed in his uniform and heave him unceremoniously into the water. He came out looking like a drowned rat, but all smiles. He took his medicine like the man he was . . . About that time, up drives Brig. Gen. Leon Johnson in his jeep, Commanding Officer of the 14th Combat Wing and holder of the Congressional Medal of Honour. Several men, with more respect than they had shown Col. Gibson, led him to the pond. He protested feebly, but knew by looking at Col. Gibson and others who had gone before, that his protest was in vain. In he went with a big splash . . . Both he and Col. Gibson endeared themselves to all personnel on the base for days. It was the talk of the group what 'good sports' they were. What a glorious day of relaxation we had enjoyed. All of us needed this break from the strain and tensions we were under.

A vitally important boost for morale was when the flying men completed their final mission. It was a celebratory time and Bob Banta recalled

I fairly bubbled at the feeling of being a grand winner. Long before the plane stopped rolling, I had unhooked all the equipment and sat on the edge of the chair ready to spring toward the waist door. The plane turned on the hard stand as I broke for the door. When the last movement faded, I swung the door open and yelled loudly to the world at large as I leaped to the ground. I took two steps to clear the exit, fell to my knees and kissed the hardstand. A photographer then recorded what had been the beginning of a wonderful life. I had been mistaken many times in the past and though I was sure I would die, I thanked God for once again bailing me out of my foolishness. The completion of our missions put an entirely different complexion on the mind and on the mood of our daily living. The thought that we couldn't look to the future without any assurance was now missing. We were alive! We could now plan and we could dream without the dark cloud of reservation.

When each man completed his missions he received a certificate making

him a member of the 'Lucky Bastard Club'. This was seen as very amusing and something to look forward to. The Lucky Bastard certificate was an unofficial document which was made similarly by each Bomb Group. They all contained the signature of the Base Commander and other senior officers.

In the end, the credit or blame for good or bad morale among a group of men lay with the leadership. It was the responsibility of the Camp or Squadron Commander to get the best he could for his men. Without doubt some failed, but fortunately these appear to have been relatively few and far between.

T.SGT. LAWRENCE RUSSOLINO SIGNING LUCKY BASTARD CLUB CHART. *(Frank Halm)*

Morale was not tangible and could not be measured statistically. It could only be measured by the will to proceed to the end and in the meantime, for life to be as bearable as possible.

FRANK HALM'S LUCKY BASTARD CERTIFICATE. *(Frank Halm)*

138

9

The Final Days

Older men declare war, but it is the young that must fight and die.

Herbert Hoover, speech at Republican national convention,
Chicago, 27th June 1944

The Allies enjoyed air superiority during the latter part of the war and intensified their attacks to weaken defences for the allied invasion. Consequently the Army Air Forces found that they were very busy during this period. 'D' Day and 'VE' Day, in June 1944 and May 1945 respectively, came and went but the war in the Pacific was to grind on until August (culminating in 'VJ' Day) and the Americans found themselves bearing the brunt of this. However, the cessation of hostilities in Europe was recognised as a hugely significant victory, and with good reason. Harry Slater remembers a sense of a great burden having been lifted:

Food, drink and dancing sprang up in every village and town like green grass in the warm spring rain. The blackout was lifted and for the first time we could see what we were doing, whether looking for a street sign or responding to the urges of romance. It was the moment when one could finally plan for tomorrow with reasonable certainty and many found themselves drifting into grateful meditation for having survived what had once seemed like impossible odds.

At Rougham air base near Bury St Edmunds, however, men were restricted to base for several days following the announcement of VE Day and Leroy Kuest felt that it was probably 'to keep us from celebrating too much and tearing up the countryside'.

Once hostilities had officially ended, the Army produced a film called *Two Down and One to Go* in an attempt to allay further speculation by the men as to what was in store for them. Everyone knew that some would be redeployed to the Pacific to engage in further fighting, but they all hoped it would not be them. In order to appear to be fair, a points system was adopted which would eventually get everyone out of the European Theatre of Operations. Points were awarded for time spent in service and overseas, for medals and for dependent children. No extra points were gained by being married. Clearing-up operations were slow. There was much paperwork to be done and air bases had to be formally handed back to the Royal Air Force. John Appleby was told that he would be leaving within the week. However:

> *Then came six weeks of frustration, annoyance and delay. Our orders were cancelled and our departure was postponed for a week; fresh orders were issued and these were in turn cancelled, so that our morale sank very low indeed. Everything on the field was closed except the barracks and the mess hall, so that we had not even a place where we could sit in comfort. We had nothing to do except the little fatigues of daily housekeeping.*

One thing that went down very badly with the British people was the fact that when the Americans left the bases, they either took everything with them or destroyed it, including food. John Bright asked his superior why they were not allowed to distribute these goods to the British and was told that it was to aid the recovery of the British economy. He saw no sense in that and disobeyed orders when told to clear out the quarters:

JOHN BRIGHT CQ SERGEANT, 95TH BOMB GROUP HORHAM. *(John Bright)*

CLEARING OUT THE BASE ON VE DAY. 93RD BOMB GROUP, HARDWICK. *(Jim McMahon)*

I was told to burn everything, blankets, clothes etc. Whilst I was clearing up I saw some young boys observing me and I knew that the British were short of blankets and clothes. I called to the boys and told them to take some of these things and hide them in the wood and to be careful to return for them after dark. They were delighted and I reported that everything had been destroyed.

Peter Ardizzi remembered an event that occurred when he heard that his base at Alconbury was closing in late November 1945:

Our quonset hut group decided to give our good, multi-channel, short wave [German] Grundig Radio to the boy who collected and delivered our laundry that his mother washed etc. When we presented him with the radio, he cried and said he could not accept it. We forgot about the registration fee and yearly licence fee to own a radio in Britain. So we passed the hat around and gave him the (paper) currency to register and pay for many yearly fees for the radio. We also told him that he and his mother, if they wanted to, could sell the radio and keep the proceeds. He left our barracks a happy boy.

Although the end of the war was what everyone had been fighting for, there was also some sadness. The weekly magazine *Picture Post* carried an article entitled 'Two Americans say goodbye.' These 'two Americans' had been in the medical corps for two and a half years and Mrs Atkinson, wife of the vicar of Buckden, said of them:

If we've been able to give them and their friends anything in the way of home life and family affection in our village, they've certainly given us gaiety while our own boys have been away . . . There is scarcely a phase of village life in which these two and their buddies have not taken part. Every week they go to the dances in the village hall – Buckden girls can jitterbug now. They go to the village charity fetes, and help with coconut shies. They have attended our church services.

BRITISH PEOPLE WAVING GOODBYE TO LAST B24 LIBERATOR LEAVING HORSHAM ST FAITHS JUNE 1945. *(USAF via Tony North)*

The crews still in Britain at the end of the war flew the aeroplanes back to the USA and cashed in on the surge of euphoria that was still going strong. Most ground men arrived home by boat and train, well after the victory celebrations had ceased, as they were needed to clear up the bases. Some were still returning home as late as 1946.

Some of the returning airmen found it difficult to adapt back into civilian life and found that they could not sit still for long, smoked more and were unable to concentrate on anything. Others, such as Harry Slater, found the experience altogether more agreeable:

When we returned home we really began to appreciate our good fortune and could better justify the things we had been called upon to do. We had anticipated great times on the town, making up for the long periods of confining duty. I do not know what the others did, but I found the rustic peace of rural Pennsylvania so satisfying that I remained at home for three weeks. This was probably an exception, but I appreciated things that I had never noticed before and savoured every minute of it. To awaken from a dream of flak and flame to the night sounds of my boyhood was a remarkable revelation of what true peace of mind was all about.

Vernon Ellis, a mechanic, vividly remembered his journey home:

Some of the ground pounders did fly home. I was one of those lucky enough to do so. After the war in Europe ended on May 8, our next objective was Japan so certain Bomb Groups were to be immediately deployed to the Far East (after picking up new aircraft in the States). The 389th was one of those selected groups. To make this move as rapidly as possible, the 'war weary' bombers were used as transportation back to the States. Ten passengers were loaded into each aircraft. Most of them were mechanics, weapon handlers, and technicians, although there were several cooks. I can say very frankly that this was the worst trip I have ever made. Only the knowledge that we were at last going home made it bearable. With ten of us on board plus the normal crew of ten, there was very little room. There were no seats. We either stood up, sat on the floor or on one of the two or three ammo boxes available. I remember that on each take-off we had to hang onto the bulkheads, gun mounts or whatever, to keep from being forced to the rear of the plane. There was no heat at all and we passengers had no flying clothing. Believe me, at 10,000 feet from Iceland to Labrador it's mighty cold on May 9. The weather was terrible, foggy, rough, and snow, sleet and hail made flying dangerous. We could not fly above it because we passengers had no oxygen equipment. There were no toilet facilities on board. To relieve ourselves we went back by the tail gun turret and 'aimed' through a one inch gap that existed between the turret and the fuselage. Usually the slip stream would draw it out, but sometimes in rough weather that didn't work and it all came back in one's face! We had nothing to eat but cold K rations, although we did eat well at each stop.

The trip was made in four legs, Hethel to Anglesey, Wales; Wales to Iceland, Iceland to Labrador and Labrador to the States. We had several days delay in Iceland when one of our fuel tanks sprung a leak. A new tank was unavailable and it was unlikely that we could get one in the foreseeable future so we found a crashed B-24 and cut open the top of the wing, removed the tank and installed it into our aircraft. It's a good thing all of us passengers were mechanics or we might not have gotten home for months. As it was I was one of the first men to get home after VE Day, before the end of May I believe. As a result I got the 'Royal' treatment. I remember the railroad conductor held back the crowd until we 'returnees' had boarded and had our pick of the seats. Two filling stations gave me gasoline ration coupons so I would have plenty of gas while home on leave. The local barber wouldn't take our money, restaurants wouldn't accept payment and it was worth your life to go to a bar for a quick beer. Before you knew it there would be a dozen drinks lined up in front or you 'on the house' or from other customers.

Frankly, I was more than a little embarrassed by it all. I didn't think I had done that much. Most of the time I wasn't in any more danger than a British schoolboy and his Nanny. Yes, we worked hard and stayed over there a long time, but my hat is still off for the combat crews. Nothing any of us gravel crunchers did can come anywhere near being shot at 25,000 ft over enemy territory.

When Bob Banta returned home, along with many other service personnel, he was sent to a very fancy resort hotel in Miami, Florida to enjoy rest and relaxation before having to return to normal life. When he did return to his hometown in Wisconsin, he was most happy about 'being able to buy milkshakes and lots of them!'

When the rush of homecoming emotions were exhausted, work had to be found and this was particularly hard on the very youngest veterans as many had little experience other than that of war.

Unlike the British, American civilians had no experience of war themselves. True, they had been involved in war work, but they had never been bombed or strafed and the V1s and V2s did not have the range to threaten American cities. Nor had the USA ever seriously been in danger of invasion and although the people welcomed their heroes back home, they found it impossible to appreciate the strain these men had endured, and expected them to readjust rather sooner than was realistic. Some made this transition more easily than others.

However, as the war with Japan was not yet over, several GIs found themselves redeployed to the Pacific. Many others were left with the physical and mental scars of war, suffering from injuries and psychological trauma that might stay with them for the rest of their lives. Some were left wondering why they had lived, and their comrades had died.

Fortunately the majority survived the war and for the young men who returned to America, their lives were still just beginning. They were now able to turn their attentions to other things, to marriage, to family life, and to building new careers and investing still further in the future of their country. Their contribution to history was far from finished.

The men of the Eighth Air Force based in East Anglia deserve recognition and our gratitude for the sacrifices that they made and their huge contribution to the defeat of Nazi Germany.

ROBERT GAMBLE, NAVIGATOR,
RETURNING HOME TO THE USA
HAVING COMPLETED HIS MISSIONS.
(USAF)

Epilogue: Remembrances

By the 1970s nostalgia for the war years was beginning to build amongst the veterans. Some had kept in touch with each other and from these on-going friendships there came a desire to re-form old groups into reunion associations. They found it pleasant to meet together, share reminiscences and to try to locate former colleagues. They sometimes visited England and their former air bases, or what was left of them, and even organised meeting up with former British friends.

The sense of camaraderie persists among the bomb and fighter group associations in the USA, although for some the memories are still painful.

One pilot ordered his crew to bail out of a damaged aeroplane which sadly resulted in the death of a colleague whose parachute failed to open.

Naturally everyone that I have spoken to has agreed that I made the only choice. We were hit at 14,000 feet and lost three engines. I flew the ship with the remaining engine to 2,500 feet before giving the order to bail out. I was lined up with an emergency landing strip, but to complete the landing would have been next to impossible under the circumstances and the rationale was that more men would survive by jumping. The radio operator, engineer, co-pilot and I all had carried out chest pack type parachutes to the plane and put them on the flight deck, in no particular order as to who had which chute. This was normal procedure. When I said that we might have to jump the engineer handed out the chutes to me, my co-pilot and the radio operator. It was just a so called luck of the draw that Craig had the defective chute.

Many of those who did not return still lie today in British soil in the American

94TH BOMB GROUP AT REUNION IN THE UK 1995. *(Leroy Kuest)*

Cemetery at Madingley, on the outskirts of Cambridge. The site was chosen because of its scenic grandeur and its close proximity to the areas where a large proportion of American war casualties occurred – in and around the airfields of Eastern England. The history of the 94th Bombardment Group included a poignant record of an observer at the official Decoration Day (now Memorial Day) at the cemetery on 31st May 1945:

I sat on a bench along the path that ran through the cemetery. I had no reason to be there, nor had I planned the trip. But for some reason I found myself there at about 10 am. The formal ceremony with the chaplain's services and the military band was very impressive, and although I had always been able to control my emotions I was quivering inside on this day. Then it occurred to me that the real drama of this day had been unscheduled and unrehearsed. I saw many young uniformed men walking down the line of markers until they found a name and number they were looking for. Then they would stop, and though every man reacted a little differently, the purpose was the same. Some would look, pause for a moment and walk away. Others stood with head bowed for a long time, and some stared straight ahead looking at the sky and sobbed silently. I wondered what brought these men here in this moment of victory. I concluded that perhaps even they didn't know. But it was likely that in the fury of battle, the death of a friend was like ammunition in that it was an expendable cost of war. Now the reality of their loss was real – and but for luck or the grace of God, it could have been them.

AMERICAN CEMETERY, MADINGLEY, CAMBRIDGE. *(D. Stuart Photography)*

J. Frank Dobie, author of *A Texan in England* (1946), visited the cemetery during the war and wrote:

> *This cemetery is on a gentle hill-slope looking far away to the east and to the north. On two sides of it are tall woods famous for nightingales singing in the spring. On the other two sides are fields that skylarks soar and sing over through spring and summer and on into fall. The sky above is a vast pathway for war planes and as I have known this spot only in wartime, they seem to me as much in place as the great flocks of rooks that stream from far places at evening to roost in the trees of Madingley woods.*

> *The land was a field tilled by a farmer who loved this plot of soil and was skilled in working it. Rows of graves and the avenues between them harmonize with the lovely hillside and the wood and the soft faraway prospect. The ground will always be beautifully kept. I have never been there without seeing fresh flowers at some of the markers and wreaths from civilians as well as from military organisations and the pedestal above which the Stars and Stripes fly at half-mast. American airmen are making the beautiful old church in Madingley village under the hill a memorial chapel. In ranks silent and orderly, row by row, recruited thrice a week, their comrades lie in a place fitting of the long peace.*

The American cemetery remains a superb monument to the American war dead and is still a huge attraction for later generations of their relatives and the diminishing numbers of veterans that are still able to make the trip to England.

After 70 years, material parts of some of the former American air bases endure, used as farm storage or some made into museums to remind us of the brave Yanks who were here. The surviving runways have grass growing along cracks in the cement and there is now the sound of birdsong and rustling cereal fields at many of the former bases which once vibrated with the clamour of war.

361ST FIGHTER GROUP, BOTTISHAM, 1986. *(Tony Stuart)*

Bibliography

Air Force Magazine. 1944

John Appleby, *Suffolk Summer* (East Anglia Magazine, 1948)

Robert S. Arbib, *Here We Are Together: The Notebook of an American Soldier in Britain* (London: Longmans Green, 1946)

Army Talks for the 8th Air Force (wartime publication)

Elmer Bendiner, *The Fall of Fortresses: A Personal Account of One of the Most Daring and Deadly Air Battles of the Second World War* (London: Pan, 1982)

R. H. Bremner et al., *The History of the American Red Cross* vol. XIII (1950)

'A Bride's Guide to the USA', *Good Housekeeping Magazine* (1945)

J. Frank Dobie, *A Texan in England* (London: Hammond Hammond, 1946)

Roger A. Freeman, *The Mighty Eighth: Units, Men and Machines (A History of the US 8th Air Force)* (London: Janes, 1986)

Geoffrey Gorer, *The Americans: A Study in National Character* (London: Cresset Press, 1955; Arrow, 1959)

Allan Healy, *The 467th Bombardment Group, September 1943–June 1945* (Brattleboro, VT: E. L. Hildreth, 1947)

Helen Johnson, Narrative Report chosen for the month of November 1944 (American Red Cross)

Charles W. Kerwood, *Assignment to Britain: An Army Forces Guide to the United Kingdom* (Washington, DC: Army Air Forces, 1942)

Norman Longmate, *The GI's: The Americans in Britain 1942–1945* (London: Hutchinson, 1975)

John McLane, *Thirty One Missions from a Navigator's Viewpoint.* 1990. Unpublished

Margaret Mead, *The Yank in Britain*. Army Talks series. (1943)

Psychiatric Experiences of the Eighth Air Force – First Year of Combat. 1944

John Magnus Redding and Harold I. Leyshon, *Skyways to Berlin: With the American Flyers in England* (Indianapolis, NY: Bobbs-Merrill, 1943; London: Hutchinson, 1944)

Keith Schuyler, *Elusive Horizons* (NY: Barnes; London: Yoseloff, 1969)

Harry E. Slater, *Lingering Contrails of the Big Square A : A History of the 94th Bomb Group (H), 1942–1945* (Murfreesboro, TN: Slater, 1980).

John Steinbeck, *Once There Was a War* (London: Corgi, 1961)

Bert Stiles, *Serenade to the Big Bird* (London: Lindsay Drummond, 1947)

US Army Air Force, *Target Germany* (New York: Simon and Schuster, 1943)

US Government agency, *Psychology for the Fighting Man* (London: Penguin, 1943)

US Government, *Assignment to Britain* (1942)

War Department, *A Short Guide to Great Britain* (Washington, DC)

John Woolnough, *Attlebridge Diaries: The History of the 466th Bombardment Group (Heavy)* (Manhattan, 1979)

Further research was undertaken at the following establishments:
    2nd Air Division Memorial Library, Norwich
    Eighth Air Force Archive, Penn State University
    Imperial War Museum, London

I would also like to expres my heartfelt thanks to my family, Tony, Rob, Doug and Annette Stuart, for contributing their various skills to this book.

Contributors

ANDERSON Bill *Ground Crew, 94th Bomb Group, Rougham*
ARDIZZI Peter F. *Ground Sergeant, 482nd Bomb Group, Alconbury*
BRIGHT John *CQ Sergeant, 95th Bomb Group, Horham*
BANTA Bob *Gunner, 390th Bomb Group, Framlingham*
BUNCH James *Technical Sergeant, 453rd Bomb Group, Old Buckenham*
CARBONEAU Dick *Gunner, 91st Bomb Group, Bassingbourn*
CLARK Macauley *Pilot, 55th Fighter Group, Wormingford*
ELLIS Vernon *Mechanic, 389th Bomb Group, Hethel*
FORSYTHE Tom *Master Sergeant, 390th Bomb Group, Framlingham*
GALIAN Chuck *Mechanic, 91st Bomb Group, Bassingbourn*
HALM Frank *Pilot, 94th Bomb Group, Rougham*
HEALY Allan *Photo Interpreter, 467th Bomb Group, Rackheath*
HIGEL Harry *Special Services Officer, 94th Bomb Group, Rougham*
JOHNSON Jim *Technical Sergeant, 95th Bomb Group, Horham*
JONES Al *Bombardier, 44th Bomb Group, Shipdham*
KOEPKE Earl, Dr *Flight Surgeon, 94th Bomb Group, Rougham*
KUEST Leroy *Ground Crew Chief, 94th Bomb Group, Rougham*
LORENZ James *Co-pilot Pilot, 466th Bomb Group, Attlebridge*
LUNDY Will *Ground Crew, 44th Bomb Group, Shipdham*
McDOWELL Bert *Pilot, 55th Fighter Group, Wormingford*
McLANE John *Navigator, 44th Bomb Group, Shipdham*
McMAHON James *Gunner, 93rd Bomb Group, Hardwick*
McMILLAN Hubert L. *Pilot, 392nd Bomb Group, Wendling*
NEWTON Fielder *Navigator, 389th Bomb Group, Hethel*

NEWTON Sam *Pilot, 91st Bomb Group, Bassingbourn*
NITCHKE Leroy *Armourer, 4th Fighter Group, Debden*
O'KEEFE (formerly FERRY) Dan *Gunner, 91st Bomb Group, Bassingbourn*
RANKIN Charles *Military Policeman, USAAF*
RUDOLPH Earl W *Bomb Disposal Officer, 306th Bomb Group, Thurleigh*
SHELLER James *Pilot, 95th Bomb Group, Horham*
SLATER Harry *Co-Pilot, 94th Bomb Group, Rougham*
WASHBURN George *Co-Pilot, 44th Bomb Group, Shipdham*

BEVANS Elsie *Suffolk civilian*
CAMBRIDGE Philip *Gunner, RAF*
FOSTER Doris *Pub landlady*
HARMONOWSKI Cynthia (née FLEET) *Norfolk civilian*
HOWARD Gilbert *Ministry of Works employee*
LANCASTER-RENNIE Jean *Red Cross worker*
LAW Joan *Essex civilian*
MAYHEW Lady *British Red Cross*
NORTH Tony *Norfolk civilian teenager*
RABSEY Judith *Norfolk civilian*
STIFF Fred and Winnie *Suffolk civilians*
STOCKWIN Nancy (née SAVAGE) *Suffolk civilian child*
WINFIELD Pamela *London civilian teenager*

Index

Note: The subheading 'quoted' indicates pages where the person is quoted but which
carry no personal information about them.

Lightning Source UK Ltd.
Milton Keynes UK
UKOW031932050712

195571UK00007B/13/P